PENGU

MAK

Judy Christy is a p................
who has had special experience with beginners of
all ages, particularly in pottery.

Roy Christy is an architect who has been successful in international competitions. He paints and is
a novelist whose books are *The Nightingales Are
Sobbing* and *No Time Like the Past*.

The authors, who are married, live with their three
children in a self-converted cottage near the river in
Fulham.

JUDITH AND ROY CHRISTY

Making Pottery

PENGUIN BOOKS

Penguin Books Ltd, Harmondsworth, Middlesex, England
Penguin Books Inc., 7110 Ambassador Road, Baltimore, Maryland 21207, U.S.A.
Penguin Books Australia Ltd, Ringwood, Victoria, Australia

First published 1969
Reprinted 1971
Copyright © Judith and Roy Christy, 1969

Made and printed in Great Britain
by Hazell Watson & Viney Ltd
Aylesbury, Bucks
Set in Linotype Juliana

To 'Bill' and Phillip Boydell

Contents

ACKNOWLEDGEMENTS

WE have had a great deal of help and cooperation from individual potters, schools of art, museums and pottery shops during the writing of this book.

Our first thanks are due to Mary Lambert who has acted as technical adviser and spent a lot of time checking the script. We would also like to thank The Hammersmith College of Art and Building for the loan of work and for the use of the studios for photographing the processes; Mr Hammond and Mr Barron of the Farnham School of Art for their willing and patient advice, and the cooperation of the pottery departments at the Epsom School of Art and the Isleworth Polytechnic.

Sincere thanks are due to the Victoria and Albert Museum, the British Museum and the Brighton and Horniman Museums for permission to reproduce examples, and Anschel of Chelsea for lending pottery.

Mr Peter O'Malley of the Royal College of Art, Mr Sydney Irwin and Mr Ron Mitchell have all given help for which we are grateful; thanks also to Miss Kidman for demonstrating some of the processes and to Mr Anthony O'Dell for his excellent drawings of various processes.

Finally, we are greatly indebted to Thomas Simmons: his skill as a designer as well as a photographer (and his wryly candid ways) saved endless discussions; his photographs speak for themselves.

Introduction

THERE are those who claim that in an industrial society the crafts, including pottery, are about to die out; they claim that they are anachronistic remnants of a former society. It is said too that easel painting is finished; painters in future must be decorators of architecture devising designs whose execution will depend upon a team of technicians sometimes working in different materials from those which the designer used. There is something to all this. It is the totality of the claim one objects to.

Certainly the great majority of things will be made industrially and no one need deny that they cannot be beautiful because of this: there is a worthwhile battle being fought to make them so. The craftsman, however, survives persistently; so does the easel painter.

Many men and women involved in either factory or office work remain creatively unsatisfied unless they design or invent something which they themselves see through from start to finish. Even professional designers, working in industry, often feel the same need, so that away from work they make things themselves. In fact, it is most probable that because the lives of most of us are spent in such small parts of a large process we turn to individual activities of all kinds – even to sailing and mountaineering – because it is here where the mind can meet a concrete reality from a certain beginning to a limited end. It is not a matter of sentiment, as many who scoff at the 'home-made gang' believe, but an important human need, very often for the most sophisticated. Pottery making fulfils this need, and fulfils it for a lifetime. It is difficult to imagine it coming to an end.

This book is not for a professional potter. It is for the beginner who starts even at home, with absolutely no idea of methods or materials for the simplest pottery, and who only later may go on to receive instruction.

Such a student, who does not know at the outset just how far his interest will take him, is quite unlikely to want to spend money on quantities of various clays, glazes and equipment used professionally or in schools. So methods are recommended for which expenditure is kept down to the absolute minimum, which may be carried out almost anywhere, and which require next to no storage space.

And this is why earthenware is chosen, why the buying of clay, advice about glazing and other matters are introduced in the simplest terms. Some of this advice, from the point of view of the experienced professional, can easily be faulted; nevertheless, it is certain that for the kind of person the book is for, these methods work, and are less daunting than more complicated ones without being amateurish or hit and miss in the worst sense.

1. The Craft of the Potter

POTTERY making is a very spontaneous matter, and this is one of its fascinations. Its shapes and decorations are often determined for ever in a matter of seconds, and once fired, are permanent enough to last for thousands of years.

Clay is the most directly tractable material of all those used in man's crafts and in this lies an immediate appeal. Wood must be carved or sawn, planed and drilled; metal beaten, cut or soldered. Clay alone may be manipulated entirely by hand, and even when a wheel is used, the hands are in direct contact with the material, finally determining the shape of the object. This ability to build with the hands, using neither tools nor machinery, has enhanced the popularity of this material through the ages.

It is clear that among primitive peoples the craft of pottery and its decoration became an important vehicle of artistic expression. In all ancient civilizations, too, when the permanence of buildings led many to be occupied with the central art of architecture, pottery still held its place among the arts. Indeed, in the writings of potters, especially in the east, it is spoken of as having almost mystical significance.

*

Damp clay is very plastic, and that is the most important thing about it. When it dries it becomes brittle but keeps its shape; that is important too. It is decomposed feldspathic rock, a mixture of silica, alumina, water, and a variety of impurities both mineral and vegetable. It is thought that the small size of the pure clay particles and their flat shape (which

causes a strong molecular attraction in the presence of water)
give the material its extreme plasticity. When heated
sufficiently the water is driven off, chemical changes take
place, the brittleness is lost and it becomes hard and
strong.

There are problems which are part of the interest and challenge of pottery making. The Ancient Greeks had pots which
cracked, the Egyptians glazes which ran, the Minoans wine
jars which were sometimes lop-sided. Indeed, the problems of
the potter are perennial and the solutions to them have not
changed. Methods have been evolved to cope with the special
characteristics of clay. Its plasticity is the most distinguishing
of these but there are also several others.

Its pliable, adhesive nature makes it possible for separate
pieces to be fixed together without the special jointing
methods needed for many other materials. Clay will also stay
in semi-liquid form long enough to be used in an absorbent
mould, but it behaves differently from other materials which
may be poured into a mould. The fact that moisture is
absorbed by the mould from the outer edge of the clay allows
the wet middle to be poured away after a certain time so that
a hollow object is quite naturally formed; also the shrinkage
of the drier outer surface permits easy removal. This last
characteristic of clay, its tendency to shrink both during its
drying time and during firing, is a property which must be
allowed for.

As a consequence of these qualities, a number of methods
for forming pottery were evolved, and ways of treating it so
that it became hard and non-absorbent. The following has
become the usual sequence of events:

The object is shaped whilst the clay is soft and pliable; at
a halfway stage between this condition and complete dryness,
when the clay is stiff but not brittle, any decoration which
involves adding more clay, and sometimes the painting, is

done. After this the pot is dried out completely. It is then fired for the first time, the clay being baked in a kiln at a high temperature, and this firing takes the clay to the 'plant-pot' or 'biscuit' stage, when the clay is hard, porous and unglazed. Next, painted decoration can be done, after which the pot is dipped in glaze and fired once more so that the glaze vitrifies. The clay has now become a decorated, glazed pot.

The methods of forming clay and treating the pottery, then, were discovered in early times and have formed the basis of hand-made pottery ever since. The methods have hardly changed during man's long progress from barbarism to civilization, during the course of many cultures, or with the comparatively recent advent of mechanization.

OUTLINE OF METHODS

It is necessary to distinguish between hollow ware of a relatively formal kind, which consists in the main of useful, though sometimes decorative vessels, and pottery of a freer type which may take the form of free-standing forms or reliefs. Although the problems which arise, and the solutions to them, are more or less the same in both cases, they are more forcibly encountered in the former kind of work.

There are two main problems – how to achieve the desired shape, and how to maintain a consistent thickness in the wall of the pot. With a free-standing model, where only the outside shape matters and bits can be added and worked into shape on a solid foundation, it is not very difficult. A hollow pot is quite different: it is impossible to arrive at any reasonable shape, certainly a symmetrical one, in this rather haphazard kind of way. Some method of controlling the making of the shape, internally and externally, must be found, for the majority of domestic pots are made symmetrical about their vertical axes. Variations may be considered for special uses but with an asymmetrical pot it is just as important to control its asymmetry.

Now to draw a freehand circle in two dimensions is difficult enough. To make a pot, out of a mass of clay, a pot whose horizontal and vertical sections must be symmetrical at any point would seem impossible – and so it is, without recourse to one of a number of traditional processes.

The simplest method is to hold a ball of clay in the hand and 'pinch' it – that is, push with the thumb until it is hollowed, rotating in the palm so that the inside shape enlarges, pressing the fingers against the outside in order to keep the wall an even thickness. As can be imagined, both the intended symmetry of shape and the equal thickness of wall can only be realized approximately using this primitive method. Nevertheless, it has been used, especially in the East, to make pottery of great quality.

The action of 'pinching', however, contains in embryo two of the most important methods of pot making. First, it resembles moulding insofar as the hand holding the clay is performing the function of a mould into which the clay is pressed. Second, when the clay is revolved in the hand to obtain the circular form it is something like throwing on a wheel.

Using a mould to form the shape is one of the earliest techniques known. Originally, damp clay was pressed into baskets whose shape and texture made it possible for the clay shape thus formed to be easily removed. Moulding has ever since been an important method in pottery making, especially if large numbers of the same object have been required as in industrial work. More recently, moulds have been of an absorbent material – soft-fired clay or plaster of Paris. With hand-made pottery, both hollow and 'hump' moulds are usually used for dish shapes. In order to make the outer and inner shapes differ, a more complicated mould which makes

14

both convex and concave shapes must be devised. Unlike the other methods moulding is a two-stage affair in which all decisions concerning shaping are made not during the actual handling of the clay but beforehand when the moulds are being constructed.

Throwing, one of the other principal methods, is absolutely direct. Clay is first spun on a flat wheel and made into a solid mass, every part of which is revolving concentrically. It is then said to be centred, ready for the second operation which is the shaping of the wall. A hole is made in the middle and, with one hand inside and the other outside, it is squeezed so that as the revolving clay passes between the hands it thins out and rises upwards. The even thickness of the wall and the inner and outer shapes are thus simultaneously controlled and if the clay has remained centred the symmetry of the form is guaranteed.

The fascination of throwing arises from the direct and seemingly miraculous way in which the pot materializes through contact with the hands. It does appear to be organically growing as the revolving clay rises from the wheel. If a wheel is not available, or an asymmetrical shape is wanted, or if the potter is not capable of throwing a very large amount of clay, then a technique known as coiling is employed. During the ancient civilizations jars of vast proportions, used for the storage of grain and oil, were built up by this method.

Clay is rolled out into long strips, the diameter of which will determine the thickness of the wall. These are then coiled into circles which are superimposed upon each other so that the height of the pot grows, layer by layer, from base to lip, and it is shaped by varying gradually the diameter of successive coils. The shape of the individual coils may be left untouched or their surfaces may be smoothed together and the whole surface treated in various ways. Very large pots are built up with thick coils which are wound round in a continuous, mounting spiral sometimes with the help of a slowly revolving wheel, the potter feeding the coils on to the pot. Coiling is a good method for building up almost any shape, including freely modelled ones when their large size makes it necessary for them to be hollow.

There is also a way of using clay in flat sheets, pinching and cutting it in the same manner as with a pie crust. The sheets may be cut up into any shape or size and may be used flat as tiles, bent into useful or decorative objects or built up and stuck together to form what are known as 'slab' pots. Sheets of rolled clay can also, very conveniently, be pressed into or over moulds.

These are basically the only methods used in hand-made pottery.

FORMS AND CHARACTERS OF POTS

Clay is a soft material which lends itself to rounded edges and subtle curves and this allows for the production of pottery of extremely varied character – one pot placid, the next dynamic and sensuous.

The Chinese pot on plate 38, its almost aggressively dramatic form shocking one in a way which normally only large-scale sculpture can do, is perhaps too disturbing for everyday life; the English jug on plate 10, ample and homely, is just the opposite; the vase on plate 28 asks to be stood on its own as a coldly beautiful form.

The ability to judge good form in pottery may be cultivated by reading and by a study of existing work, but there is no doubt that all who have had practical experience have a greater awareness of what is apposite to the material. They will see better when slight departures from symmetry aid the rhythm; will appreciate the subtle simplicity of one form as opposed to the crudity of another. These and many other aspects of pottery may become alive to them. As a student of the famous Japanese potter Shoji Hamada has said*:

... He seemed unashamed of his materials, letting them have their head, not imposing his will on them ... through him I really became aware of my materials. I became as interested in throwing and turning and decorating as in the things themselves ... throwing marks up a cylinder, or the coil that swirls from the centre of the bowl, the shavings from turning.

Facility of technique is not everything, however. The late Classical Greeks, for example, produced pottery which is well-shaped but is somehow lifeless [plate 15]. It is something to do with the drawing which, lovely though it is, would be more suitable to a flat wall than a pot – but this is not all. Some Egyptian stone jars nearby in the same museum may supply the answer. They are similar in shape, have the same hard, thick edges, and, one realizes, the shapes are apt in stone but not in clay.

If the material is of crucial importance so is the function. For a piece of hand-made pottery to fulfil its purpose the precision made possible by industrial methods is not necessarily an important criterion. Note the asymmetry of the Chinese pot in plate 28, and how this is just what humanizes what might have been a rather cold object. Absolute symmetry has no intrinsic merit if other qualities are lost or missing. Indeed, perfection, some ancient Chinese potters thought, was an attribute proper only to their gods, and if by chance a pot was finished without fault, it would somehow be made imperfect.

Yet real functional considerations are of vital importance, and have often determined the basic shapes of pottery. There is positive enjoyment, for example, in a shape which balances

*Pottery Quarterly, No. 29, 'Ways of Working and Thinking', by Brian Newman.

properly in the hands, fits the fingers, pours without spilling, and retains its lid in the process.

The material and functional elements of pottery making are the challenge from which most of the world's great pottery has been created.

2. Pottery Without a Wheel

THE beginner is advised to buy prepared clay (plastic not powdered) from a commercial pottery, or from a potter's supplier who will offer a number of clays firing at various temperatures. One red and one white clay should be bought, firing between 1080°C and 1150°C, and, should there be a choice within this range, avoid those recommended for making casting slips. It is better to start with the red clay which has a pleasanter texture than the white and is easier to work. A cream or white surface can be given to a red pot with slip or opaque glaze (see chapters 4 and 6).

A few potters dig their own clay, others prepare their own mixtures, but most buy from a merchant – sometimes making slight additions to alter it (usually to coarsen it). To explain why the prepared clays are normally used and the reasons for recommending particular ones it is necessary to give some technical information about clay.

Natural clays are either found where they are originally formed (primary clays) or where they have been carried by water or sometimes ice and wind (secondary clays). The second kind will have decomposed more and will have collected various organic and mineral impurities. The original clay particles and the impurities will have become smaller and more intimately mixed the further they have travelled. This fineness of particles gives greater plasticity to clay and causes greater shrinkage in the firing. The impurities act as fusible elements (fluxes) which means that in a secondary clay there is a higher proportion of material present which melts at low temperatures.

Although secondary clays can be, and have been used in their natural state there is such an immense variety that the chances are extremely small of finding one that is easy to work, fires at the right temperature, and does not shrink or warp too much in the process. Primary clays are rarely suitable for use in their natural state because of their lack of plasticity and the shortage of fluxes in the composition, and in fact are used only as ingredients in other clays.

Various local clays have special qualities and may be mixed with others which lack them. Of the primaries in England, kaolin or China clay from Devon or Cornwall will give whiteness and increase the firing temperature: of the secondaries, the Devon and Dorset ball clays are useful for increasing the plasticity of a clay that is too short, that is, not sufficiently plastic.

Clays dug from the surface of the ground usually contain too much organic matter and other impurities for immediate use. Clay must in any case be cleaned and matured before it can be used for anything but the most primitive kind of pot; it must be exposed to the weather for some months, then reduced to a slip and sieved – all of which is lengthy and impractical for a beginner. It is, however, interesting and valuable to try firing local clay, and provided that the temperature is not high (say 1000°C) some sort of low quality pot can often be achieved.

Potters' merchants supply different kinds of prepared clays suitable for various types of work; these are mixtures (sometimes very complex) of different natural clays and other substances, and they are often called 'bodies', especially in industry. Before these clays can be described, three technical terms must be defined:

FUSION – means melting. When the unmelted components in the clay can no longer support the melted ones, the clay collapses; this is termed in pottery 'complete fusion'. In fact, all the components would eventually melt if submitted to a high enough temperature and when cool, would form a kind of glass.

REFRACTORY – the ability to withstand high temperature. A refractory clay has a comparatively small proportion of fusible elements.

VITRIFY – to become glass-like. A vitrifiable clay is a refractory clay which melts enough to become dense and non-porous before collapsing. Some bodies are fired to a point where vitrification is just beginning, others until it is almost complete.

Potters' clay falls into three types:
1. *Earthenware clays*

These clays are divided into two groups:
(a) Clays which have a maturing temperature below 1100°C. and contain a high proportion of fusible material, and can be used for slipware, Majolica unglazed pottery, or for young children's work.
(b) Clays which mature between 1100°C. and 1150°C. – the kind recommended for the work described in this book. There is not sufficient refractory material present for vitrification to take place before the clay collapses, so that the fired body is always porous unless glazed. This is also true of industrial earthenware bodies which are often fired at higher temperatures.

2. *Stoneware clay*

This matures between 1250°C. and 1300°C. It is vitrifiable, which means it is non-porous at the maturing point.

3. Bone china and porcelain bodies

These fire from 1300°C. to 1400°C. or even more and are usually too 'short' to use without special methods. Only an extremely experienced potter would consider using them. A high-firing porcelain body owes its translucent quality to the fact that it undergoes almost complete vitrification and fusion.

Earthenware is recommended for beginners because of the relatively greater problem of firing stoneware.

First, there is the kiln. Those who become really interested will want their own at home and for earthenware, electric kilns of reasonable size and price can be simply plugged into the normal domestic current, and pottery up to 15" or 16" high may be fired. For stoneware, to have one firing anything larger than 8" or 9", there would have to be a more expensive kiln needing a high ampage intake, or a gas kiln requiring special intakes and flues.

Second, because stoneware is fired at a higher temperature it has to withstand greater stresses, the likelihood of breakages and other disappointments is increased, especially with the work of a beginner. There is also a more restricted range of colour for decoration.

ESSENTIAL EQUIPMENT

Clay

At least ½ cwt of red clay and the same of white will be needed. These can be stored separately in plastic bags or in plastic or galvanized buckets with lids. A damp cloth should be kept inside the containers to make sure the clay does not dry.

Working surface

A piece of unvarnished, close-grained wood is needed to work on; a pastry board, a piece of deal, the old-fashioned kitchen table, or even off-cuts of block board or plywood will do. Non-porous surfaces such as Formica or Fablon are not suitable as the clay will stick to them.

Clay cutter

The wire cutter (figure 1) is almost like a cheese cutter – that is, a piece of wire or nylon thread with a handle at each end. To make a wire one, cut off about 18″ of brass picture wire

Figure 1. Wire cutter

(local hardware shop) and unwind two or three strands. For the handles, two 4″ lengths of lath, pieces of old ruler, old-fashioned clothes pegs, or any similar pieces of wood will serve. Loop the ends of the wire round the middles of the pieces of wood (notches or holes in the wood will stop the wire from slipping), so that the wire is double for about 1½″ of its length at each end; hold the wire and turn the wood so that the two strands of wire twist firmly together; push the end back towards the handle so that it will not scratch the hand. Nylon fishing line may simply be tied round handles to make an adequate cutter; it lacks the bite of twisted wire, but is stronger.

WEDGING

Before clay can be used at all it must be prepared by a process called wedging. This is very important as it ensures that the clay is free from air bubbles and is of even consistency, both conditions being essential if the shape of the pot is to be controlled and if it is to be successfully fired.

Some potters prepare their clay by kneading or by wedging and kneading. As this requires greater skill it is not recommended for beginners.

Take a piece of clay weighing between 3 and 4 lb, bang it on the edge of the working surface, tilted so that the wire will slide beneath it and cut it in half (plate *a*); roll the front piece upwards and over until it rests on the top of the other, the two cut faces towards you; pick up the top piece (plate *b*) and again bang it heavily on to the other so that the two pieces flatten into one, and all the air is squashed out of the joint (plate *c*); turn the whole lump upside down as well as through an angle of ninety degrees, slip the wire beneath it and start all over again. If the lump gets untidy pat it into shape again.

Clay which is new from the shop will need wedging ten or twelve times, but previously used clay will take longer.

TO MAKE A THUMB POT

Take a lump of red clay about the size of a tennis ball and roll it on the board or table until it is more or less spherical. Cup it in the left hand, press the right thumb into the centre to make a hole; then, gently rotating the ball of clay in the left hand, squeeze the clay between the right thumb on the inside and the right fingers on the outside, by which method the walls of the pot will start to form and become thinner and taller as you work (plate *d*). Go back to the bottom of the pot in order to squeeze the clay from there up to the top, until the wall is too high to do so. Then finish as you go.

There will be a tendency for the top (or lip) to crack, especially if it has been over-handled or if a too dry clay has been used, and these cracks must be smoothed away immediately by gently stroking the clay together. However, a feeling will quickly develop for the right consistency of clay, neither too dry nor too wet, and this makes all the difference to the ease with which it can be modelled.

Finishing

As soon as the walls of the pot are about ¼" thick, and all cracks have been removed, stop working the clay and flatten the bottom by holding it in both hands, tapping it on the table top. If the rim is at all untidy it is possible to remedy this by wetting the fingers of both hands and then, while holding the rim between the first finger and thumb of the left hand, to rub round the whole rim with two fingers of the right hand. If the fingers tend to pluck out clay, dampen them again so that they slip easily over the surface. Almost all beginners, as soon as they have realized that a little water helps, are tempted to spread it over the whole surface, for indeed a temporary and superficial effect of smoothness may be attained fairly quickly in this way. Resist this temptation or a little later the clay may become unworkable and the shape may collapse. Work with clean, damp hands throughout. Pull together any superficial cracks with the fingers and always support the pot with one hand when working with the other, or it will be pushed out of shape.

Types of thumb pot

The size of the pot is, of course, limited by the amount of clay that can be contained in the hand, and in the main only bowl-like, thick-walled shapes are possible because of the difficulty of controlling the clay accurately. Ash trays, sugar or bulb bowls, and so on, can be made. The Japanese Raku-ware tea bowl illustrated (plate 1) is an example which, although it is not perfectly shaped, has a certain sophistication; the slight inward curve of the wall, where one might expect a straight surface, gives an unexpected liveliness.

Purpose of this method

It is possible that when the student has progressed to other methods he may never again want to make a thumb pot. Nevertheless, it is an excellent start, for if clay has never been handled before there is no better way of finding out how the material behaves. Particularly the amount and kind of handling it can take will be appreciated, as well as its strength in the plastic state. Pots made in this way are sometimes a little crude, but are hardly ever lifeless.

A COILED POT

Coiling opens up much greater possibilities, for a great variety of objects, from the size of an egg cup to a really large jar, can be made in almost any shape. It is wise, however, to start with something medium-sized as both small and very large objects have their own special difficulties. A pot like the one illustrated (figure 2), approximately 9″ high is a suitable beginning.

The Base

Make a ball of clay about 2″ in diameter and, working on a piece of thick paper or canvas so that the clay does not stick to the table, form it into a flat disc about ⅜″ thick. In order to do this bang the ball four or five times with the edge of

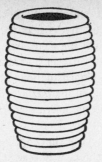

Figure 2. Coiled pot

the hand, and again the same number in a position at right angles to the first; rotate the clay between the hands but on the table, pressing it into circular shape; turn it over and repeat the process for another sequence – and so on, as often as is necessary, until the disc is 5½″ in diameter (plate *e*). If at first it is difficult to bring about a proper circular disc then find a suitable plate or saucer to sit on the shape formed and cut away the superfluous clay with a knife.

Coils

For this pot a series of worm-like coils of clay of about ½″ diameter should be produced. To do so take a fairly soft piece of clay and shape it roughly to resemble a cigar, smoothing away any bad creases and cracks. Using the working top, roll the clay with long, even movements of both hands, starting from the middle and working outwards; as the coil lengthens keep it thinning equally moving the hands to the fattest part, noting that the centre tends to thin more quickly than the extremities (plate *f*).

Avoid too great a downward pressure or it may be found that, instead of the coil rolling smoothly under the hands, it bumps unevenly. If so, parts of the section will have become oval. If this happens pat it gently until it is round, and start rolling again, very lightly. It may be that the coil gets too thin in places, in which case it will be necessary to start again. Having got the coil even and round, it may crack when it is bent to form a ring if too long has been taken and the clay has dried too much, in which case there must also be a fresh start with another piece of clay. Where the ends of coils become hollow, they should be pinched off.

It is important to keep the working surface clean: use a damp cloth unless the clay is very soft, when a dry one is better.

Building up the shape

Start to build up the sides of the vase, ring upon ring of coils. Have a small bowl of water to hand and wet the outside edge of the top of the base with the fingers, as with the edge of a pie before putting the top on; this is done for the same reason in both cases, simply so that what is put on will stick to the base. Lay a coil on the circumference of the base, nipping off the ends if necessary, so that it forms a ring slightly wider in diameter than the base, and join the ends carefully with a little water so that the ring is quite even. Dampen the top of this, and, having rolled out more coil, lay upon it another ring, very slightly larger in diameter than the first, making sure that the joint occurs in a different position. Take a good look from the top to see if the plan of the pot is remaining round and hold it up to eye level, turning it about to make sure it is rising evenly and not growing lop-sided. If the rings are going at all wrong they must be removed in order to correct the shape, so keep a constant check on the profile. It is most important, whenever joining pieces of clay together, to see that they are firmly pressed into each other, otherwise, as they dry, they may break apart; the ends are best cut diagonally and overlapped rather than butted together.

Joining

After two or three rings have been made they must also be joined more securely on the inside. To do this, support the outside with the left hand, and, with the thumb or nail of the first finger of the right hand, drag a little clay from one coil to the next, all the way round with downward movements, making especially sure the bottom coil is joined to the base (plate g). Then run the pad of the finger tip round and round the inside of the pot to make the surface smooth and neat. As with the thumb pot, resist the impulse to wet your hand to get the smoothness: once again, though it seems to help at first, the pot will become so soft that it will start to distort.

The pot can now be built up by laying ring upon ring, varying the diameter of the rings gradually according to the desired curve; the last ring may be a bit fatter so that it is firm and rounded, completing the pot. A useful aid to shaping is a template cut from cardboard which can be placed against the profile as it grows. Plate 31, although illustrating a thrown pot, shows a good shape which it would be possible to make by continuing with coils of diminishing diameter.

Finishing

The outside surface must now be finished. It is smoothed in the same way as the inside, by dragging the clay from coil to coil so that the hollows between them are filled up. On the outside it is possible to work from the top to the bottom in one movement, remembering to support the inside with the left hand while working, but, if any hollows or thin parts remain, damp the area and fill in with an extra piece of clay. The shape can also be improved, and the pot strengthened, by gently beating the outside with the back of a tablespoon or the handle of a knife after it has hardened a little.

The pot could now be decorated in different ways but these

will not be described until chapter 4. If it is not to be decorated it can simply be left to dry out, but if when dry the
surface is still not entirely satisfactory it may be smoothed
down with fine sandpaper. Always rub with a circular motion
so as to avoid making flat areas. The objection to rubbing is
that it may result in a lifeless surface.

Pots of all sizes and shapes can be made in this way by
altering the diameter of the coil – large, tough-looking garden
pots; elegant, slender ones like modern Swedish jugs; small,
delicate cruets – though the smaller ones require greater
accuracy in making.

The large, monumental pot in plate 2 was made by coiling.
Part of its robustness is due to its bold surface texture and
this was simply achieved by dragging the coils together with
the fingers, as described, sometimes pinching in extra pieces
of clay. Plate 3 shows two coiled shapes whose surfaces have
been smoothed off and afterwards decorated with coloured
glazes. At the other end of the scale plate 46 includes an oil
and vinegar set no more than 4″ high, showing that it is
quite possible to make fairly delicate things by this method.
Plate 4 shows a truly remarkable coiled pot by a twentieth-
century African potter working in her own highly skilled
native tradition: at first it is hard to believe that it is hand-
made, so perfect are its contours. From accounts given of her
demonstrations in England, she works in a way approaching
ritual, almost dancing her way to the conclusion of the
pot.

TO MAKE A SLAB POT

Various pots of an angular character can be made in this
way. The following instructions are for making a simple box
which could be used for plants.

Extra equipment

Some more simple equipment is required – a wooden rolling pin or equivalent piece of wood about a foot long and three inches in diameter, an old knife, a piece of natural sponge, a ruler and set square, or anything that will give a right-angle. Several pieces of strong paper will be needed – cartridge or thick brown paper – not newspaper or shelf-paper, which will tear and stick to the clay. Even better is some stiff canvas or sacking.

Mixing clay and grog

It is better to mix some 'grog' with your clay, which prevents shrinkage and warping in the drying. This is a powder made of already fired clay which can be bought by the pound from a pottery, or any of the large potters' suppliers. A white one of about 80 mesh is satisfactory.

To mix clay and grog together, take about 8 lb. of clay and cut it into slices about ½″ thick with the wire cutter, wet each piece and cover with grog, pile the treated slices on top of each other, and wedge as usual only even more thoroughly. The water may make it rather sticky at first but it is absolutely essential to counteract the drying action of the grog.

Rolling out

Now roll out the clay on a piece of the paper with a rolling pin, just as with pastry, until it is ½″ to ¾″ thick, freeing the clay from the paper during the rolling process. Then, to get the clay absolutely flat, take a piece of smooth wood, a wooden or a steel ruler, and, holding it on edge with a hand at each end, drag it across the clay surface, first in one direction then another. Keep removing accumulated clay from the edge with a damp cloth.

Cutting out

Mark and cut out the pieces of clay as shown in the diagram (figure 3).

Trimming

Finally, the pieces must be trimmed a little in order to straighten the edges and square the corners. This, however,

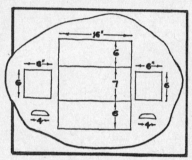

Figure 3. Marking out flower box

must not be done until the clay has dried somewhat so that it is hard enough to keep its shape but is not yet brittle. This condition is said to be 'leather hard'. At this stage drainage holes may be punched in the base with an apple corer.

Slurry

The slabs are now ready to be made into the box, the adhesive used for this process being 'slurry' – a rough mixture of water and clay. For small quantities this can be made by rubbing small pieces of the wettest clay you have between your fingers in a little water, or by collecting pieces of absolutely dry clay, crumbling them and mixing them with water.

Making up

Take the base, still on its piece of paper, and put it on a rigid board, or anything flat and firm; so that if the work must be moved it may be picked up easily. Peel the paper off one of the side pieces, score the bottom edge as well as that part of the base to which the side is to be stuck and apply slurry to the edges. Fit the two pieces together as in the diagram and rub a finger along the joint, on the outside, to make sure it is flush; hold it for a minute to see whether it shows signs of falling or sagging. If it does either, quickly make two or three thick rolls of clay with which to prop it

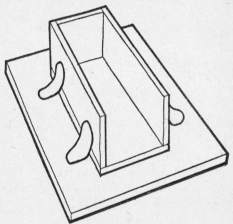

Figure 4. Making the flower box

back from the outside. Next, fit into position the two end pieces in the same way, making sure there is plenty of slurry between the surfaces which contact each other (figure 4). Before fitting the last side it is wise to do any tidying up of the inside which might be necessary. Finally, each joint should be strengthened from inside by working a small coil of clay into the angle.

Finishing

Work on the joints of the outside walls with fingers and a damp sponge until the surface is smooth and neat, and the line of the joints is invisible. If the long sides show a tendency to bow, smooth them straight with the hand or a piece of wood; if the top edge looks too hard and square, scrape away the sharp corners with a knife and smooth with the fingers and a damp sponge.

Handles

Open handles can be made by the simple expedient of rolling out two coils of clay and attaching them to the ends of the box; they might however, appear feeble in form against the solidity of the trough and another idea for a more robust handle is proposed.

From the rolled out clay, cut two pieces shaped like the sectors of circles, about four inches long and an inch wide at the deepest point as illustrated (figure 3). Bend the tips downwards so that each shape becomes an even curve with about 2½" between the two ends, in the same way as before stick the flat end on to the short end of the box about 1½" from the top, one handle at each end, and work them firmly on. Make a coil about ¾" in diameter and stick lengths of it along the outside edge of each handle, finishing the coils neatly by smoothing them into the sides of the box: the coils will give the handle a rounded edge, substantial-looking and practical (figure 5).

Some kind of pattern on the long side might make the trough more interesting. Decoration is not discussed until a later chapter, but the sort of effects that may be obtained by impressing, carving or adding pieces of clay can be seen in plates 4, 8, 9, and 11. If decoration is decided upon the trough must be prevented from getting any drier. (How to do this is described later in this chapter.) Chapter 4 will indicate some ideas concerning design and decoration.

Although the slab method may at first seem very limited, it is surprising what a range of pottery may be made by it.

Plate 5, a simple but very striking large example, shows the effectiveness of sharp arices contrasting with surface texture; plate 6 shows smaller scale work of a softer quality, and

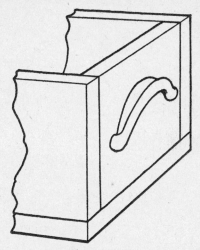

Figure 5. Flower box handle

in one of the examples curved slabs are used; plate 12 illustrates pottery thrown on a wheel, but shapes similar to these could be made by pressing slabs round solid cylinders. Empty Vim powder cartons with the ends cut off can be used to make mugs. Newspaper is wrapped round the carton so that the clay will not stick to it; the mug is finished with a base and handle. Finally the carton is removed and the newspaper carefully peeled off.

THE MAKING OF TILES

Tiles can be made with the same mixture of clay that was used for the slab pot. Roll out and flatten the clay in the way previously described, cut it into 4½" or 6½" squares, and trim the squares when they are leather hard, by cutting along a straight edge.

Drying out

As clay dries it shrinks and tends to warp if it does not dry out absolutely evenly. Flat pieces are particularly prone to curl up at the edges so tiles should be put to dry away from direct heat and draught, and turned over from time to time. With tiles of ⅜″ thickness or more there should be little difficulty, but if thinner tiles are needed, they should be stacked in piles of four or more, a slight weight placed on top, and left to dry, very slowly.

If tiles are sliced from a block of clay rather than rolled out and cut up, there is less danger of them warping. For this method a special tool is required: it is a U-shaped piece of rigid metal with a piece of fine wire or strong nylon thread stretched taut across the open end. The bow should be about 8″ × 12″ and the distance from the ends of the metal to the

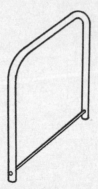

Figure 6. Tile cutter

wire should equal the thickness of the tile required. (See figure 6. Most suppliers stock this tool or it can easily be made by a handyman capable of bending metal.)

Make the clay into a block, the base of which should be a little bigger than the tile required, and high enough to cut as many tiles as desired. Hold the tool with the ends on the table, and, making sure they slide along its surface, drag the bow towards you through the clay block: should the block slip, either get someone to hold it or stand it close to the table edge and pull against the stomach. Accurate tiles can be made quite simply by this method.

The real interest of tiles lies in their decoration which can be done in many ways, either with different coloured slips (see chapter 4) or by painting before or after the first firing (see chapter 5).

BENT CLAY WORK

Possibilities of this method

The use of sheets of clay as the basis for making pottery calls for imagination and ingenuity. The method involves cutting out shapes from rolled out clay and bending them to make such things as plates, decorative plaques, and simplified or wholly abstract ornaments. It is very like paper sculpture carried out in clay so it is as well to experiment with paper first and use a full size paper pattern for cutting out the clay.

Making a plate

To make the rectangular plate illustrated in figure 7, roll out to the required thickness the same sort of clay used for slab pottery, cut the corners as shown in figure 8, turn up two adjacent sides, score the joint and stick with slurry. The turned-up edges may need the support of coils of clay while drying. Repeat this for each corner.

The lion illustrated on plate 43 gives an idea of the kind of small sculpture that might be made in this way. The head, front legs and feet have been modelled in the round, but the

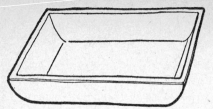

Figure 7. Plate of bent clay

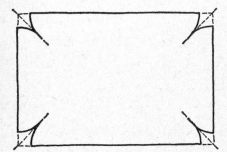

Figure 8. Pattern for plate

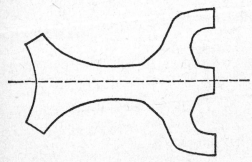

Figure 9. Pattern for lion

main body appears to have been cut from a sheet of clay and bent; figure 9 shows how the shape might have been cut.

Although the model of a horseman on plate 41 is not made entirely of bent clay it owes a good deal of its character to the use of it; coat and hat, tail and harness are all made in this way.

Combination of methods

It is, of course, possible to combine some of these methods in the making of one pot: coils, for instance may be used for developing a thumb pot, or for adding a neck or a foot to a slab pot.

MISCELLANEOUS FACTS ABOUT CLAY

Keeping unfinished work

Unfinished work and pottery waiting for certain types of decoration must be kept damp and undamaged. If the work is small it can be stored in a polythene bag, sealed with a rubber band and placed on a board so that it need not be handled every time it is moved. Alternatively it may be put in a large biscuit tin with a damp cloth inside which should not touch the work itself. Eventually a 'damp cupboard' will be needed – a metal-lined cupboard with slatted shelves, a water tray in the bottom, and tightly-fitting doors.

Joining new work to old

If there has been an unavoidable interruption in the making of a coiled pot it is likely that, when work is resumed, the last coil will be drier than the new one and special care must be taken. The surface of the old coil must be roughened and well damped so that the new one really marries with it.

Damping

If a partly finished piece of work does get too dry it is possible to dampen it by holding under the tap for a second, allowing the water to soak in and repeating as necessary. Alternatively, it may be sprayed with clean water using a garden spray or something similar. It is usually impossible to retrieve a pot which has become bone dry; at this stage it will crack and even disintegrate if it is wetted.

Re-using dried clay

Any pieces of clay that get too dry can, however, be used again, and it is wasteful to throw away all the odd lumps which accumulate. They can be soaked in water and dried out on a plaster slab (see chapter 3), to the plastic state, wedged and re-used. An enamel or plastic bucket or bin makes an efficient container in which to soak the dried clay. Any larger pieces should be broken up first by hammering them in a sack.

*

Many students, once they have started throwing on a wheel, entirely give up making pottery without it, as though hand-built methods were only for learners. This is a great pity for, in the past and today, pottery of great quality has been made without a wheel. Indeed, many experienced potters return to hand-built methods from time to time, creating work of much greater subtlety than when they were students.

Shapes can certainly be formed more quickly on a wheel and they will have a different character from those discussed in this chapter. But hand-built pots have a quality of their own; sometimes more sculptural, more static than thrown pots, they are every bit as appropriate to clay.

Equipment used in making the objects described in this chapter:

Working surface
½ cwt white clay
½ cwt red clay
1 lb. grog (80 m. white clay)
Polythene bags
Wire cutter
Rolling pin
Old kitchen knife

Small basin or bowl
Natural sponge
Old ruler
Set square
Board or tile for keeping
  work on
Pieces of thick paper or canvas

Useful extra equipment:

Covered rustless buckets
Plaster slab
Biscuit tin

Tile cutter
Damp cupboard

3. Plaster and Simple Moulds

THERE is another simple way of forming clay for which a mould is required. Something reasonable might be made by taking half a grapefruit skin or coconut shell, and by evenly pressing soft pieces of clay over the inside surface.

For more advanced work it is essential to use a mould made of superfine white plaster, obtainable from a pottery supplier. Unless a personal visit is made the plaster is often only supplied in hundredweights. However, dental plaster, sold in 7 lb. tins at larger chemists is an adequate substitute. Keep the plaster dry and do not stock it for more than twelve months as it deteriorates. An air-tight biscuit tin or small dustbin is suitable for storage.

When plaster is mixed with water a creamy liquid is formed which takes about ten minutes to set, during which time it expands, and when hard retains the shape of anything it is poured into, so that the most minutely detailed modelling is reproduced from the mould. Used as a mould for clay it assists the drying of the pot because it is extremely porous.

The detail of Rococo statuary or of Adam's eighteenth-century ceilings gives an idea of the refined character possible with plaster and also demonstrates its durability. It is also possible, as always, to misuse it horribly – witness most modern Catholic statuettes, and 'pot' dogs.

MIXING PLASTER

To mix the plaster pour almost enough water to fill the mould into a bowl and, with a dry hand or a spoon, sprinkle the plaster slowly on to the water; it is best to sift it through the fingers to avoid lumps, scattering the powder over the water surface evenly, adding until small islands of dry plaster start to form on the surface. Leave for a minute, then mix the plaster and water into a smooth liquid. 24 oz. of plaster to a pint of water is a suitable mixture.

It is most important that the mixing is done quickly; setting starts as soon as the powder gets wet, and, as the process only takes ten minutes in all, the mixing must be done quickly or lumps will form. Try to avoid lumps or air bubbles, for removing them will cause serious delay. For all these reasons it is better to do everything with the hands – both sprinkling and mixing. To mix, put a hand in the bowl, fingers spread flat, and shake it from side to side.

The chief points to remember are:

1. Have a big enough bowl.
2. Put plaster into water, not water into plaster.
   (Try the wrong way, just once.)
3. Be quick, and be careful of lumps and air bubbles.
4. Don't mix until all the plaster is in.
5. Don't go on and on stirring the plaster as this will prevent it from setting.

Two further points. First, if surplus plaster is being poured down the drain make sure it is mixed with lots of water and that plenty is flushed after it. Second, put waste bits of set plaster into the dustbin straight away, for if any bits get into clay which is to be fired, they will expand in the firing and crack the work.

With care it is quite easy to make plaster, though it might be best to practise on something unimportant the first time. A small plaster batt, useful for drying out clay or standing work on, is a simple thing to make.

Making a small plaster batt

To make a circular one about 8″ in diameter, mix 2 pints of water with 48 oz. of plaster in a bowl and allow it to thicken, pour on to a piece of glass, letting it pile up until it is roughly 2″ thick and, when set, slip it off the glass. If the last operation is difficult pour water over it or put it under the tap; it will come easily then. Alternatively, the plaster can be poured into a plastic washing-up bowl and allowed to set.

MAKING A MOULD FROM AN EXISTING POT

The simplest way to make a mould is to use an existing pot as the master shape. Open dishes or bowls with an absolutely smooth glass or glaze surface would be best. Only a pot which does not narrow towards its top, and which has no concave sections can be removed from its mould. (See also chapter 10.)

The articles needed are as follows: a suitable dish, plaster, water, and a bowl for mixing, as well as about 12″ of galvanized wire, a piece of reasonably tough cartridge paper for making the handle, and an old knife.

Make sure the selected pot is clean and stand it on a horizontal surface. Then take the wire and bend it into a loop as shown in the illustration (figure 10); roll the paper into a cylinder 4″ or 5″ long and about 2″ in diameter, securing the seam with sticky tape or paper clips.

Mix the plaster, banging the bowl gently on the table so that air bubbles rise to the surface and burst; fill the pot with plaster, banging it in the same way for the same reason. Just as the plaster begins to set push the wire loop into the middle a fair way, making sure it is not touching the bottom or sides, and hold it there until the plaster has set rigidly around it (figure 10). As quickly as possible, mix enough plaster to fill the paper cylinder, score deeply the plaster round the base of the wire to make a key for the next mix of plaster, put the

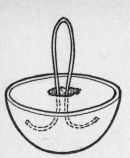

Figure 10. Making a mould. Wire loop in position

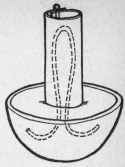

Figure 11. Paper cylinder in position

cylinder over the loop and, holding it firmly on to the surface, fill with the new mix which should be just thickening but still pourable (figure 11).

In half an hour this should have set hard, whereupon the paper should be peeled from the handle and the mould removed from the pot. The mould may be found to stick, so go carefully; trying running water round the edge to break the suction and, if absolutely necessary, slip a thin knife round the side, watching carefully to avoid damage. When the mould is out, bevel off the sharp edge with a knife, making a facet about ¼″ wide at 45 degrees to the side (figure 12). The mould must thoroughly dry out before it can be used and this will take about twenty-four hours. Do not hurry it by putting near the fire; a warm cupboard is better.

Repairing a mould

An air bubble or a rough patch on the surface can be removed – the patch by rubbing round and round with very fine sandpaper, the bubble by blobbing thin plaster into the hole with a soft brush and sandpapering afterwards. Neither remedy is entirely satisfactory.

Figure 12. Finishing the mould

MAKING A PRESSED POT

Roll out enough clay to cover the mould adequately, put the mould on to the centre of it, trim off any surplus and then, holding the mould handle in the right hand, slip the left under the clay and paper on which it was rolled and turn them over. Gently press the clay over the mould, for which action it will be easier to hold the mould in the left hand. Then peel off the paper without disturbing the clay (figures 13 and 14).

The next part is very important. The clay has to be coaxed into assuming the shape of the mould without pleating and whilst maintaining an even thickness. With the ball of the hand, working from the middle outwards and down the sides, press the clay so that it thins slightly (plate h). A flat rubber tool called a 'kidney' may also be used for final smoothing. Some of the excess clay can be cut off with the blunt edge of a slim knife or a large hatpin, but beware of tearing away more than is intended. Continue the pressing until, when

Figure 13. Pressed dish. Mould placed on clay

the mould is turned over, there is no tendency for the clay
at the sides to fall away from it, and trim off surplus clay

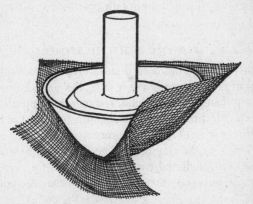

Figure 14. Peeling off the backing

from the edge as before, holding the knife edge along the
bevel to finish neatly (plate i). A slight push should remove
the clay from the mould. Should the clay be soft allow it time

to harden a little. If the edge is rather sharp, run a damp finger round once or twice until it is properly smoothed, otherwise afterwards the glaze might not adhere and there would be a rough lip. Plate 6 shows some decorated pressed dishes.

MAKING A MOULD OF ORIGINAL DESIGN

It is far more satisfying to make a mould of one's own design and this can be done quite simply.

Any open, non-undercut shape (that is, one without any concave sections, which could not be removed from a one-piece mould) is suitable. (Again see chapter 10.) It may be round, oblong, oval, multi-sided, regular or irregular, so long as there are no sharp angles (knife-like ones make the pressing of the clay almost impossible), and it has enough flat base to stand on. It is possible, of course, to have a rounded or keel-like base but this will mean putting a foot on afterwards.

MAKING A HUMP MOULD

When the shape has been decided draw on paper, full size, the plan of the rim and cut it out. Now get a large lump of clay and bang it into a solid, rectangular lump about 1½" bigger in all three dimensions than the pot about to be made. Put this on a rigid board and score round the paper shape on the surface of the clay block. The chosen shape can now be scooped out. Skill and patience are needed for this, because the shape must be smooth and even so that the pot will be too.

The beginner could use the fingers or a simple tool such as a spoon or a blunt knife. Two modelling tools are useful at this point – one with a wire loop, the other with a flat, round end. The wire one is for scooping out the clay and the other

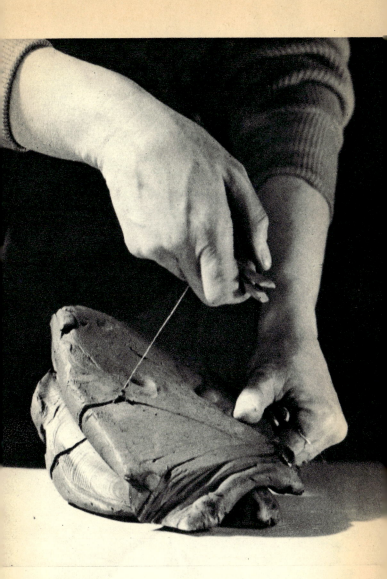

a. Wedging

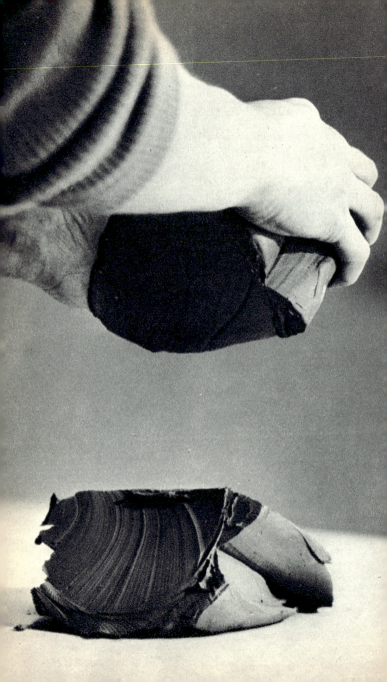

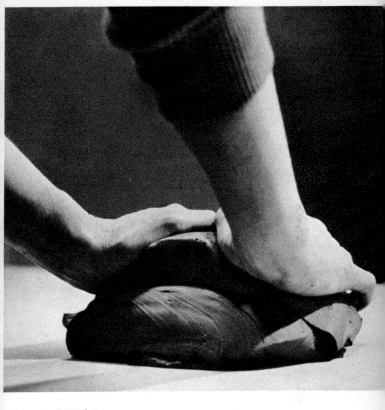

b. (*opposite*) Wedging
c. Wedging

(*opposite*) Making a thumb pot
Coiled pot. Making the base

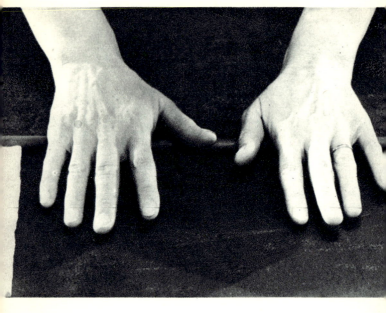

f. Making a coil
g. (*opposite*) Joining coils

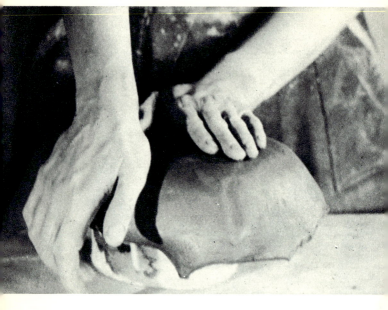

h. Pressing the clay over the mould

i. (*opposite*) Trimming the edge

j. (*opposite*) Throwing. Wetting the clay
k. Raising the cone

l. (top) Flattening the cone
m. Centring

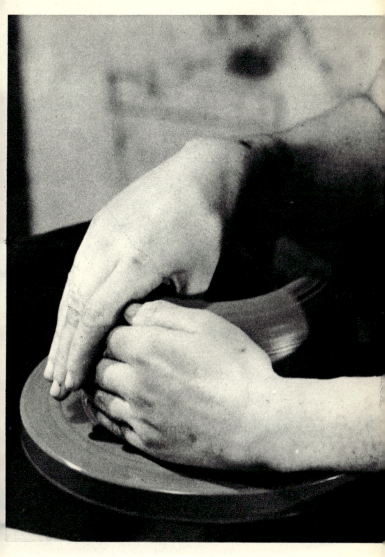

n. Making the hole

o. (*opposite*) Raising the wall
p. Basic cylinder

q. Collaring

r. Finishing the rim

s. (*opposite*) Finishing the foot
t. Cutting off the pot

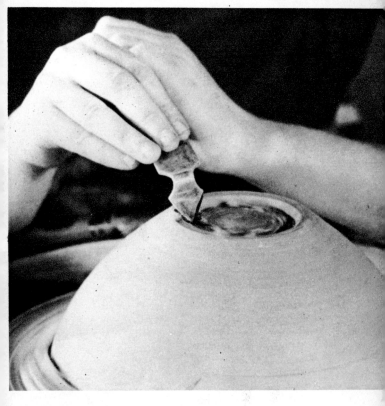

u. (*top left*) Turning. Flattening the bottom
v. (*opposite*) Trimming the outside edge
w. (*above*) Shaping the foot

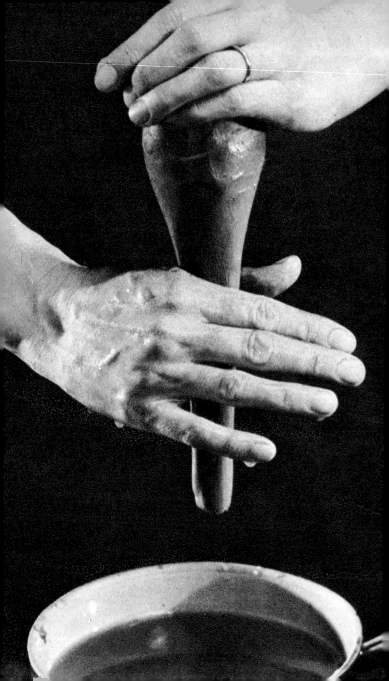

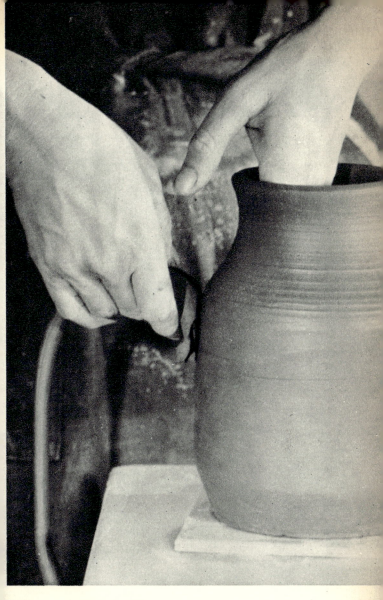

x. (*opposite*) Pulling a handle
y. Placing a handle

z. Pulling a lip

for smoothing the surface. Smoothing is comparatively simple; the difficulty is to get the surface even. Use the wire tool, having hollowed out the main shape, working over the

Figure 15. Master shape for hump mould

surface in all directions, not in one only, for this makes the surface even more irregular (figure 15).

When the shape is finished, make the mould in exactly the same way as previously. Before returning the clay to the bin wash off any plaster sticking to it.

MAKING A HOLLOW MOULD

A hollow mould, the opposite of the *hump* mould, is frequently used for pressed dishes. This type supports the clay as it dries, which is useful for larger shapes. Since the clay shrinks away from the mould it is easy to remove, and unlikely to crack as it would if left too long on a hump mould.

To make one, the master shape is modelled upside down, as a solid lump, on a large board. Clay walls are raised all round the shape about an inch away from it, in order to contain the plaster which will be poured over it, the walls being made from rolled out strips of clay about 1″ thick and 1½″ wider than the height of the master shape. The strips are used on edge, joints firmly stuck together, and clay buttresses must be spaced outside the walls to make sure the plaster will be held (figure 16). When all is ready, plaster is poured over the master shape until it is covered by at least 1".

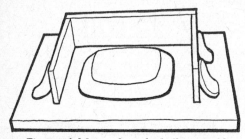

Figure 16. Master shape for hollow mould

Have some pieces of clay ready to plug up any leaks which might occur. When dry, the clay is removed, and the mould is ready for clay sheets to be pressed into it. The walls for large moulds are stronger if made of pieces of board whose corners are held together with clay.

Making a plaster batt

As mentioned earlier a plaster slab for drying-off clay is a useful piece of equipment; this can also be made in a dress box or something similar, and is better reinforced by some galvanized wire netting.

Mix sufficient plaster to fill the box to a depth of 3" and pour it in, shoring the sides with bricks or anything heavy enough to give adequate support. When the plaster starts to set, press in a piece of wire netting about 2" smaller than the box all round, making sure that it isn't touching any exterior surface of the slab. When it has set peel off the box and bevel the edges with a knife so that plaster does not flake off into the clay being used.

*

Much more complicated moulds, consisting of many separate pieces, can be made, and are widely used in industry for the manufacture of jugs, teapots, vegetable dishes, free-standing models, and so on. There is a description in chapter 10 of simpler piece-moulds.

In making pottery with either simple or complex moulds, there is always the same split between design and execution, a split which does not occur in other methods. Every pot will have the shape and character that the designer has given it, whoever makes it. With hand-built and thrown pottery, though the shape is fixed in the mind before it is begun, the form develops as the potter handles it.

The need for an extremely calculated approach to the design of moulded pottery gives a distinctive character to it, obviously less alive and direct than that of other pottery, more intellectual than instinctive.

Equipment used in making the objects described in this chapter:

Superfine white plaster of Paris	Cardboard dress box
Wooden modelling tool	Galvanized wire netting
Wire modelling tool	Galvanized wire
Bowls for mixing	Cartridge paper
Knife	Paper clips or gum strip
Spoon	Fine sandpaper
Pieces of glass or smooth	Soft brush
surfaced board	Kidney

4. Decoration Before Firing

ONCE the form of a pot is determined, the texture, the colour, and especially any pattern applied to its surface further establish its uniqueness. The single, particular decoration can have more meaning than the mechanically repeated one.

The 'body' of stoneware pottery and the glazes used with it can have real qualities in themselves as decoration: with earthenware it is different. A simple, glazed earthenware pot, however fine its form, has a negative surface which seems to demand decoration. And this is why so much successful earthenware has been vigorously decorated either with clay or with painted colour.

The same design principles apply to all pottery decoration; so the two chapters on it are placed together – even though clay decoration takes place before firing, painted decoration usually afterwards: it is also why use is made of painted examples in this chapter.

There are two main modes – the purely abstract, and another in which natural forms have been rigorously stylized: the Chinese Neolithic pot (plate 37) exemplifies the former; a modern plaque (plate 24), the latter. It is thought that early man decorated naturalistically but that constant repetitions resulted in abstract simplifications. Be that as it may, the overwhelming majority of successful work throughout history has been done in these two ways, the second again and again proving an even more fertile style than the first – the purely abstract.

The formal volumes of pottery do not need – in fact, seem

to be mutilated by – an excess of three dimensional realism. Naturalistic decoration has been successful (almost always when it covers a small proportion of the surface – as in much eighteenth-century enamel painting on porcelain) but it has spoiled more pottery than it has improved. The ample shapes of eighteenth-century jugs are frequently decorated with excellent portraits which yet detract from their striking profiles.

My enthusiasm got out of hand when I decorated. I painted every surface in sight and some that weren't. This seemed to be a way of getting a pot to come alive, so that it became more than just an austere, cold shape, modest and unassuming. I had, and still have, an ambition of making a pot where the form and decoration are equally important, not one dominating the other.*

Brian Newman has here made articulate the ambition of many a potter. Almost nothing concerning pottery is more exciting than this challenge.

There are many ways of decorating clay while in its soft state; marks may be indented or pieces added – sometimes in clays of differing colour. But nothing may be altered after the clay has been fired. Once clay is handled for this kind of work, ways of carving pieces out, or of pinching and bending the clay in the fingers, come almost instinctively. Although these methods are the most primitive, the carving technique, for example, was developed with great refinement in Chinese and Persian work.

There are also more complicated ways. In 'sgraffito' the whole surface of the pot is coated with a thin covering of differently coloured slip (see p. 57) which is later scraped back to the original surface for the decoration. Or there is a kind of cake icing technique, known as slip trailing, which was used most vigorously by eighteenth-century

* *Pottery Quarterly*, No. 29, 'Ways of Working and Thinking', by Brian Newman.

potters, and, more recently, by artist potters such as Bernard
Leach and Michael Cardew. A method in which clay is cut
away or stamped in, and filled with clay of a different colour
inlay was used very effectively in medieval tile designs.

All these ways may be employed to produce decoration
which is intrinsically part of the object it is covering.
Although decoration can be painted on unfired work it is
more convenient to describe it together with other types of
painted decoration in the next chapter.

IMPRESSED DECORATION

The simpler methods – impressing, pinching and generally
making indented marks – are akin to pastry decoration, and
are sometimes used for the same functional reason, that is,
to help stick two pieces of the material together whilst
decorating simultaneously. Coils of a pot can be drawn together with impressed patterns made with fingers, keys, pen
nibs, forks, spoon handles, etc. Geometric patterns or images
of natural objects may be executed on the surface of any pot
either by drawing with an instrument or repeating a series of
indented marks, or a combination of both; the lips or feet of
pots can be pinched into scallops. All these methods have
been used over the centuries.

One or two home-made tools may be helpful at this stage.
A roller to be used for patterning can be made simply by
forming a cylinder of clay with a hole down the middle, and
inscribing a pattern on its surface. When it has been fired a
piece of wire can be threaded through it and bent to make a
handle (figure 17). Useful small knives are easy to make from
broken hacksaw blades sharpened on a grindstone.

The slab pots (plate 6) show the effectiveness of a simple
repetitive impressed pattern. The fish on plate 42 has been
delightfully decorated (probably with a knitting needle) with

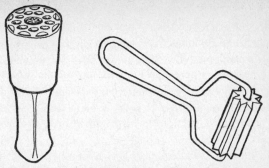

Figure 17. Roller and stamp for impressed decoration

circles of varying scales, and lines suggesting fins: such decoration sets up a flicker of light and shade over the main form. The distinguished pot on plate 36 shows how a serrated blade may be dragged across the clay to create texture: in this case the contrast of the two textures is the main idea of the decoration.

CARVED DECORATION

With a small knife or lino cutter decoration can be carved out in low relief. Coloured glazes will tend to stay thicker in the parts cut away, thus enriching the design. The background can be textured with an impressed pattern, coloured with slip or paint, or just left plain.

Carved decoration of a primitive but effective kind is exemplified in the Aztec pot (plate 8). The clay was cut away cleanly so that there are two distinct flat planes playing against each other: this flatness accords with the severe angularity of the composition. The rounded Persian jug (plate 9) shows very different carved decoration: contours were formed by carving and engraving so that the decoration was rounded into the surface. In all examples the method tends to produce a sculptural effect.

RAISED DECORATION

Raised decoration made with applied coils and pellets of clay has been used repeatedly. Stamps may be found, or made from clay, by which pellets may be patterned, much as the wax seal was impressed by the signet ring: coloured glazes can be flooded into the folds of coils, like cloisonne. All raised decoration must be applied with slip which acts as the adhesive.

The modern breadbin (plate 11) is a confident shape in itself, but it is greatly enlivened by the well-organized rhythm of suns and wheat ears (made up of small coils of clay pressed together). It is a large example, and it would seem that this type of decoration is better for bigger-scale work (as with much medieval pottery, for instance), otherwise it only tends to look like a flaw in the smooth line of the profile. Nevertheless much of the smaller-scale Wedgwood ware is successful because it is made from a fine textured clay which makes possible a high degree of refinement.

PREPARATION OF SLIP

Slip is a form of clay which has been frequently mentioned for it is constantly needed in a pottery for both making and decorating. There are two ways of producing it. The first method is to bang lumps of dried-up clay with a hammer or mallet to produce powdered clay which is soaked, and then sieved twice so that it has a smooth, creamy consistency. The second method is to sieve sludgy clay from the waste bucket in the same way. A stiff brush, a sieve and two stout sticks (or two strips of angle-iron) are required, the latter spanning the rim of the bucket with the sieve resting between them. A potter's sieve is a wooden cylinder with a bronze 'lawn' stretched across it about a third of the way up. It is numbered according to the number of holes per linear inch; for slip a no. 80 is needed. The sieve is used with its deep end uppermost and only partly filled with slip to prevent it slopping over the edge. The slip must be stirred vigorously with the brush and soft lumps may be pushed through with the thumb. The sieve and contents are banged down on the sticks from time to time to clear the holes.

Storage

Making slip is a rather long and dirty job so it saves time to make a fair quantity: both the red and white varieties are always useful and should be stored in covered buckets. It should be stirred thoroughly at least once a week, for if the clay particles get packed at the bottom it is sometimes necessary to resieve the slip to have it smooth again.

Oxides for colouring slip

Mineral oxides are used for colouring slip, and these can be bought either raw or as specially prepared body stains. The stains should be used with clay bought from the same suppliers and should be mixed according to their instructions. (See Appendix, pages 125–7.)

The raw oxides recommended are: cobalt (a strong blue colour), manganese (purplish-brown), copper (a good green which sometimes tends to spread in the firing, and, if too much is added, turns a metallic black – a colour which is pleasant but not green), lead antimoniate for an opaque yellow (this is poisonous until fired), and iron oxide (a rather browny-yellow). A mixture of cobalt and copper makes a turquoise, one of cobalt and manganese with red slip a very dark brown or black.

The final colours must not be expected when the oxides are first mixed with the clay, for, in fact, most of them will look a dirty grey: it is only after the first firing, sometimes, indeed, not until the glaze firing, that the true colours come out. Copper carbonate looks nearer the final colour than copper oxide and for this reason is probably less confusing for the beginner to use.

Preparation of coloured slip

The colour is prepared by mixing the oxide with a little water, allowing it to soak, and then sieving it through a fine 100 mesh sieve. Cobalt has very hard particles which remain as specks in the fired pot unless crushed by grinding the colour with a palette knife on a tile, with a pestle and mortar, or by sieving it through a 200 mesh sieve.

The colouring and the slip are now mixed, the proportions being, roughly, a dessertspoonful of colour to a pint of slip for pale colours but as much as four or five to a pint for strong ones. The strengths of particular oxides vary: cobalt and copper are strong, lead antimoniate and iron oxide weak, and manganese is about the norm. For precise recipes see notes on the uses of oxides for colouring. (Appendix, pages 125–7.)

Decorating with slip

It is first necessary to coat the surface to be decorated with a thin covering of slip, and this must be done when the pot is leather hard or it may become too damp and collapse. For the same reason it is unwise to coat both the inside and outside of a pot at the same time.

When coating the inside of an open shape with slip support must be given to prevent sagging. This is done by making a nest of coils which closely fits the underside of the pot and rests solidly on the baseboard (figure 18). Another method of preventing the pot from collapsing is to dry it, before the slip soaks it, in a warm cupboard or fairly near a fan.

For the outside coating the pot is held by the foot and is

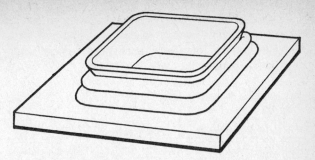

Figure 18. Dish supported with coils

dipped upside down in a bowl of slip. Air pressure prevents the slip rising inside. Another way is to hold the pot the right way up, fingers pressing outwards from the inside, and dip it up to the rim: this method avoids all finger marks. For the inside, the pot is half-filled with slip, rolled around until the slip just touches the edge all round, and the excess is poured out. In both cases a twisting shake will get rid of any surplus slip which would otherwise dribble back and spoil the surface. If there is any kind of error it is unwise to try and touch things up: it is essential to sponge all the slip off, to allow the pot to dry, and start again. The first experience of a pot properly covered in slip is very satisfying.

Sgraffito

Slip a white pot with red or a red pot with white, allow it to dry again to leather hardness, scrape a design in the slip so that it reveals the colour beneath – and a 'sgraffito' decoration will have been made. This is a very direct, exciting method to use. The design can be a tracery of thin lines or a series of contrasts between lines and areas cut away: and the lines may be of uniform thickness or fluidly thick and thin as in script writing, for which purpose a chisel-shaped tool is used. Using all kind of objects as tools – a big nail filed to a chisel end, a screwdriver, a knitting needle, a wooden modelling tool, and so on – experiments can be made with varying combinations of line and colour mass.

Slip trailing

What is called 'slip trailing' needs greater skill but has a singular fascination. Slip is forced through a nozzle (described in the next section) and 'trailed' on a wet, slip-coated surface. There is no time for doubts or hesitations, and any accidental blobs or misses have to be incorporated into the design. It is impossible, in fact, to work out and carry out a design without experimenting first. The designs will have to be simple and large-scale, distinctly formalized whatever attempts may be made to the contrary, because of the nature of the method. The tip of a feather or a fine point swept across parallel lines of slip will produce a chequered effect: marbling effects may be achieved by tipping the pot about so that different colours get mixed up.

Trailed decoration will normally be slightly raised, and only a pressed dish permits absolute flatness. Then the flat, rolled out clay must be pre-decorated so that the trailing is flattened out when the dish is pressed. The added advantage of this is that there is no possibility of the slip 'slipping' as it sometimes does on a steep side.

The Thomas Toft plate (plate 17) is not a first-class design, but it shows the range of possibilities in the technique. It is 17¼" in diameter as the rich treatment of the mermaid's hair and tail, and the rim could not be executed on a smaller scale. Plate 18 illustrates a very convincing design of traditional character carried out by a contemporary amateur: plate 7 shows a variety of pressed dishes with flat, slip decoration, again the work of amateurs.

Slip trailers

The only special tool needed is a slip trailer. One type is a thick rubber or plastic container, bulb-like, with a glass or plastic nozzle in the end. To operate squeeze the air out of the container (without its nozzle), put the open end in the slip, release the pressure so that it fills itself, and replace the nozzle. Another type of trailer has a soft, flat bag with a nozzle but this is more difficult to fill though less inclined to 'spurt' than the other. Still another is rather like a baby's bottle with two open ends; one end has a cork with a quill pushed through it, the other a hole to blow through. This kind may sound difficult to use because the trailing is actually done by moving the head around and blowing; in fact, it is surprising what accurate control of the flow of slip can be achieved. It was used by the seventeenth-century Staffordshire potters, the earliest examples being made of fired clay.

Trailers can be purchased from pottery suppliers or, if necessary, a small ear syringe bought from a chemist is a reasonable substitute.

STENCILS AND RESIST

Another way of decorating is to use some sort of resist which prevents the slip sticking to certain areas. This can be done with paraffin wax, warmed and diluted with paraffin and brushed on the surface, or by sticking thin paper shapes, leaves or even flowers to the clay. The pot is then covered with slip and when this has set the paper or leaf is pulled away and the wax melts at the firing stage. The character of the decoration done by the wax resist method is fluid, that achieved the other way is stiffer and more incisive. (See plate 13.) Decoration started like this can be developed with engraved or trailed lines. Slip may be painted on, but it is important that it is done fairly thickly, for what looks solid at this stage tends to fire away and even completely disappear when glazed.

Inlay

Coloured slip allowed to dry on a plaster batt becomes coloured clay: this may be used, for example, for inlay decoration, a type mentioned earlier in connexion with tiles. A pattern stamped into or cut out of clay with a knife or lino cutter is filled with the coloured clay, and, when all is dry, the surface is scraped flat with the edge of a knife.

Difficulties

Technically all these methods are fairly simple, and provided the slip fits the body and is of the right consistency for the particular method there should be no difficulties. A little experience will soon show the correct thickness of coating for 'sgraffito'; one which is too thin will lose its strength in the firing especially if it is lighter in tone than its ground. Should white slip applied to a red body tend to peel off, ball clay must be added to the white slip (25 to 50 per cent). Both should be weighed dry, in powder form, if accuracy is desired.

Design

It is difficult to be brief on the subject of design. The student undergoes a slow maturing, and insight comes in all sorts of ways – through books, study of examples and by reflection – but most of all, through practical application rather than from the formulation of general theories. Nevertheless, it may be possible, especially with the use of examples, to make a few points which will help in the design of pottery decoration as a whole, even though this chapter is mainly concerned with decoration in clay.

The primary aim is to achieve unity of character between

the pot and the decoration. The carved decoration on the Aztec pot on plate 8 is exactly in accord with the pot itself; both are straight-lined, angular, tough. The factory-made eighteenth-century jug (plate 14) is a failure; decorated with an unsuitable engraving it simply illustrates that, where liberty has triumphed, design sense certainly has not. The decoration and lettering are badly placed and the lunette decoration looks like a hole in the jug.

There is a much greater possibility of unity when the pot is made and decorated by the same person, and it is interesting to remember that in the last example two entirely separate persons were involved. Plate 15 shows a beautifully-shaped classical Greek pot: here a painter has decorated another craftsman's pot, producing elegant painting more suitable for a flat mural than a rounded pot.

There should also be unity between the form of the decoration itself and the shape of the pot, whether the design be abstract or formalized. Both these types of decoration may be used in different ways: first, there may be an individual design located on the pot with sufficient undecorated surface around it for its effect to be particularly insistent; second, there may be a somewhat repetitive design which more or less covers the whole surface; third, something between the two extremes – a type where a main shape is surrounded by smaller scale decoration so that there is a dominant mass on an all-over background.

The first way is exemplified on plate 16 – an eighteenth-century earthenware dish with sgraffito decoration. It is a strikingly bold linear design whose curves are always brought into harmony or counterpoint with the rim of the dish. There are other qualities too: the apparently casual cross-hatching on the bird is absolutely essential to its dominance; the spaces outside the motif are as important a part of the whole as the spaces within. The design of the rim, however, is comparatively weak, the thinness of its line out of scale. The painted decoration on the Chinese pot in plate 32 is finely related to the shape. Spare, but eloquent, the curved brush-strokes take up the form; the dark base holds the pot down. The horizontal rings divide the shape into horizontal sections at significant points and stabilize the curves; there is a particular satisfaction in the way some of the brushstrokes challengingly spear at the rings.

Plate 45 shows an elegant, slip-cast jar, perfectly plain but for the lovely decoration of small doves in the recessed circle; its severity makes the slightly sentimental decoration quite acceptable.

The Persian bowl (plate 19) and the English jug (plate 10) have very different qualities but both illustrate the more overall type of design. The bowl is an example of deft brush-work rhythmically moving over the whole surface, naturally contained within the shape. Its success depends partly on a contrast of scales – very important in this type of design; the main lines of the foliage curve round the dish from edge to edge, throwing off smaller and smaller branches which almost always finish in a small, fine curve. The most ineffective type of overall design is that in which a small scale motif is monotonously repeated. The jug (plate 10) has a sgraffito decoration used in a more or less overall way; again there is a range of scales right down to the small dots forming the background and the decoration is stabilized by the dark base and rim, as well as the rings placed at the lower junction of the handle.

The Persian jug with sympathetically rounded, carved decoration (plate 9) shows the third way : there is a combination of a main motif, the bird, with a background of smaller objects, so that the whole surface is carved in relation to the profile. The plain base and plain, purposeful collar and handle are an effective contrast.

The Thomas Toft plate (plate 17) also has one main motif combined with smaller ones. It is a likeable enough plate in a naive way, but the twist of the mermaid's tail and the flow of her hair do not manage to unite the stiffly vertical body with the rest of the design: what is more, the too closely patterned slip on the rim tends to destroy the dominance of the central theme. The modern dish (plate 18), again an example of slip decoration, is not so technically accomplished, but is better as a complete design.

The Spanish plate (plate 21) is magnificent: the designer has courageously taken the form of his deer straight over on to the rim, even touching the edge several times; the curves thrust at it or run round with it, the leaves assisting the movement; in the background, more reticently, the rhythm is elaborated on a smaller scale. Though the plate is designed to be seen especially one way up, it is almost as satisfactory any other way, because, as in good heraldic design, the form of the animal and the surrounding spaces have been equally considered as abstract design.

*

Whenever rigid classifications are made in visual matters, satisfactory examples can be found which do not fit the categories. The breadbin on plate 11 is one such, where the decoration consists of alternating motifs set on a plain surface, the decorative handle helping to unite the whole. It is useless to attempt a complete grammar of design, for rules may sometimes be broken, expertly, with complete success.

Equipment and materials used for decoration

Slip
80 mesh phosphor bronze lawn (sieve)
100 mesh sieve. (Also used for glaze, chapter 6)

Stiff brush for sieving slip
2 strong sticks
Bowls or buckets
Slip trailer
Metal Oxides for colouring slip – 1 lb. of each :

Cobalt oxide   Lead antimoniate
Copper oxide   Iron oxide
Manganese oxide

Prepared oxides or body stains
Fine knives
Lino cutting tool

5. Painted Decoration

SUCCESSFUL pottery painting, more than painting in any other medium, depends on sympathetic brushwork in addition to design. The brush may be used so skilfully and economically that each stroke is a decorative form in itself (plate 29); it may produce a rhythmic flow of thick and thin lines with the sudden contrast of a fine, deft twist; or small descriptive painting using tiny strokes.

Painting has also been misused again and again; almost every style in history has been imitated in miniature with tremendous skill but with little sympathy for pottery, and the museums are full of examples – pots covered with Chinese or Dutch landscape, Rococo erotics, or eighteenth-century conversation pieces – all examples of misapplied labour and cunning. Nowadays the freer styles are being abused in a sloppier and cruder way.

*

DECORATING BISCUIT-FIRED POTS

Painting on a biscuit-fired pot is similar to water colour painting on very porous paper. The pottery brushes are made of long sable or camel hair; the colour is transparent. The porous biscuit immediately takes the colour from the brush so that each stroke, with its accidental lights and darks, will have its own identity. This sort of painting is very direct and the painter must not be tentative or hesitant; everything must succeed the first time. It is a most exacting but rewarding art, and readers who have tried a direct method of water colour painting will have experienced this kind of satisfaction.

The shape of each mark is made in a continuous stroke controlled by the pressure and movement of hand and brush. The Chinese have always excelled at this and a Chinese painter had to undergo a long period of instruction and practice in brush strokes before he attempted to depict anything with them. In fact the traditional method was to do many studies for a painting before the final one was executed extremely quickly, but not so artlessly as might appear. Brush-stroke practice is a good discipline for anyone, and certainly each design should be tried out on paper before executing it on the pot.

Tools and materials

The equipment needed consists of brushes, a palette knife, a tile for grinding, and gum arabic or tragacanth for use in the mixing water to prevent smudging. The basic metallic oxides used to colour slips are also used for painting: 'underglaze colours' listed by suppliers are made from mixtures of these and other metallic oxides. The number of colours offered can be overwhelming for the beginner who would do well to consult the list at the end of the chapter. (See also Appendix, pages 125–7.)

Mixing the colour

The colour is in powder form and has to be mixed with water and a little gum. Gum can be bought from the chemist in lumps or crystals and has to be mixed by shaking up with hot water – about a teaspoonful to a quarter pint; this will keep in a screw-topped jar but it will tend to smell unpleasant after six or eight weeks. To mix the colour take enough powder for the job in hand, grind it to a thick paste with a little water, and add a drop or two of gum. Thin the mixture with a little more water as it is used, more or less according to the porosity of the surface to be painted. The gum prevents the colour from running when the pot is dipped in the liquid glaze, but too much will cause bubbling during the glaze firing. It is disconcerting to find that the colours before firing frequently have not the slightest connexion with the name on the packet. (Willow blue is an ash grey, blue-green a dingy green.)

Making a sampler

Because of this it is a good idea to make a sampler, that is a piece of biscuit tile or pot on to which can be painted small patches of every colour as well as any mixtures which may be attempted. (Mixtures are not normally recommended but are sometimes successful.) This tile may then be glazed and fired, so that in future the finished colours are predictable.

Of the colours available, the blues, greens, browns, yellows and black are reliable, but scarlet, crimson and pinks are very uncertain as their colour is easily burnt away in the firing. Generally speaking the colour should just cover the pot so that it dries matt and solid-looking, but since some of the blues are stronger they should be thinned before use. Reds, on the other hand, should be applied more thickly. The necessary thickness also depends on the porosity of the biscuit, so try an experimental brush mark on the base of the pot.

Although the paint looks opaque while in use, it becomes transparent when fired : this means that, as with water colour, a light tone, such as yellow, will not show over a darker one like blue. It must also be remembered that the colour of the body affects the colour of the paint, just as the paper does water colour. Only the darker tones, therefore, will show on red clay, and then not in their true colours.

Banding

To paint an accurate band round a pot it is necessary to have some sort of turntable (a gramophone will do). Make sure the pot is exactly in the centre, load the brush with colour, and hold it still with the tip pointing in the direction in which the wheel is moving, just touching the revolving pot. The freehand method is less accurate but useful for pots of uncertain symmetry; hold the loaded brush in the same way, and draw the line round the pot while the little finger keeps in contact with the edge – the whole hand being rigid so that it acts as a compass.

Guide lines

Sometimes it is necessary to have a guiding line or marks to help space a continuous pattern; use a hard pencil faintly and sparingly because its marks will not always fire away, and it is no good trying to rub them out. Moreover, the colour itself will not wash off completely if a mistake is made, though hard scrubbing will erase all but a slight stain of most colours.

Stippling and spraying

Colour may be applied by spraying or stippling with a sponge or cloth; both are useful ways of covering or texturing large areas and can be used in conjunction with a wax resist.

Painted decoration on unfired work

The same colour can be painted on to unfired work before it has become completely dry. Since the surface is usually less absorbent than biscuit it is easier to paint on; also mistakes can be scraped off. This last fact may be used deliberately and decoration of an engraved character can be created. Because the brushwork need not be so rapid and sure, painting on unfired ware is less daunting for a beginner.

Decoration on tin glaze

Tin glaze (described in the next chapter) fires an opaque white. It is the glaze traditionally used for painted decoration of peasant pottery (Majolica, Delft, etc.) for two reasons. First, the glaze will cover any coloured clay, thus providing a white surface which gives brilliance to the painted colour; otherwise, only white bodies prepared for industry can approach this. The glaze slightly alters the colour, making copper more blue, iron more orange, and manganese more purple than when applied direct to the body. Second, a tin glaze runs less than others during the firing, so that the decoration hardly moves.

The decoration is painted on to the glaze before it is fired and when it is 'set' but not quite dried out, so that the surface is not too porous for fluid strokes. The glaze surfaces must be smooth and even. The basic metallic oxides or underglaze colours must be mixed with water; too much will cause dribbling and flooding, too little an interrupted brush stroke. If the pattern is close handling may smudge the paint, so a few drops of gum should be added to the water to fix it. Very small alterations can be made by scraping off and retouching but this is difficult, so if the painting is spoilt in some way it is better to remove the glaze and start again.

Enamel painting

The most delicate painting of all is done in a third way with enamel colour on a pot which has received its second firing, and which is then fired again, after painting, at about 850° C. More colours, including gold, silver, and various lustres can be employed, because of the low-firing temperature.

Most commercial tableware is decorated in this way; the more expensive is still hand-painted but most mass-produced pottery is decorated by means of applied transfer. It allows very precise work, and some extremely beautiful painting has been done, especially in the eighteenth century, not always well related to the pot, but which even the most obdurate purist would find hard not to admire. As enamel colour is painted on the hard surface of the fired glaze it is mixed with an oily medium and this lends to the method being more suited to small, even miniature, decoration.

Application of enamel paint

Enamel colour is mixed with a special oily medium and ground with a bone spatula on a tile, after which it is thinned with genuine turpentine or a proprietary thinner. The gold and lustre colours, which are expensive, come ready mixed and need no thinning; it is essential to use clean, dry brushes or the colour will not fire properly.

As most hand-made pottery does not have a fine enough surface to be really suitable for enamelling, plain, glazed ware can be bought to decorate. The pottery should be clean and free from dust, and dirty marks should be rubbed off with whiting on a dry cloth; no water must be used as any damp penetrating into the body will cause 'spit out' (an unpleasant, rough surface when fired).

*

DESIGN AND BRUSHWORK

It might be as well at this point to refer to the end of chapter 4, for many of the remarks made there apply to both clay and painted decoration. (Consistency of character between pot and decoration; unity of decoration and shape; variations in scale in the case of an overall design, etc.) Beginners whose brushwork is not yet fully controlled can still achieve bold line or rich pattern and decoration of great charm. The following comments are concerned mainly with brush techniques but also with design in painted decoration.

The Persian bowl (plate 19) has already been mentioned and it is a fine example of design and brush technique: the strokes narrow and widen, ending sometimes in a thin coil or a round blob as the brush was retracted; the main lines are continuous strokes executed without raising the brush.

The painting on the twentieth-century Spanish plate (plate 20) is quite different in character and technique. Short strokes, not varying very much in thickness, have been overlaid to produce a pattern which is more solid than open, softer in its edges, yet no less vigorous. Unlike the rim of the Thomas Toft plate criticized previously, this one has just the right density of decoration to allow the central design to have its say.

It is impossible to resist mentioning the English Lambeth plate (plate 22), a splendid example demonstrating yet another type of brushwork. The paler washes would have been applied first with a broad brush and the thinner lines overpainted with a finer one. In a homely way it is an authoritative design, spontaneous yet controlled.

The examples on plates 23 and 24 are many years apart (the first by an early Greek potter, the second by a modern designer and amateur potter) but they make an intriguing comparison: they should be an encouragement to those who are not naturally spontaneous with a brush, for they both have painted decorations whose characters, though different, depend upon a carefully designed drawing which is lined over with a brush – all motifs, patterns, lettering and textures executed with slow precision. Note that the banding on the bowl occurs just below the handle junction.

Plate 37 shows the work of a neolithic Chinese potter. Here is a lovely form impressively decorated with an abstract pattern. The painted curves harmonize with the profile of the pot and the decoration ends where the curve of the profile eases into a straight line, at which significant point the handles are placed; the edge of the darker decoration is soft-ened by a wavy line, the light-toned rings bring the upper part into relationship with the lower; only the painting of the rim is perhaps a little out of scale.

The examples on Plates 20, 21 and 22 illustrate the softer edge obtained when painting on tin glaze; the others, the harder lines produced by painting on biscuit.

In the majority of examples illustrated the decoration has been limited to one colour (used against a plain background), the dish on plate 21 to two, and that on plate 22 to three. Throughout history, beautiful painted pottery has been achieved with only one or two colours; much Victorian work and some Italian Majolica ware show the dangers of using too many.

Most of the painted examples are from the work of the past, for most present-day professional potters (for whatever reason) work in stoneware and their pots are often treated with different glazes where the effect is one of colour varia-tion rather than individual decoration: even when the dec-oration is painted on it is often so like the pot in tone that the result is similar.

Tools and materials mentioned in this chapter

1 fine sable or camel hair brush
1 large sable or camel hair brush
Palette knife or bone spatula
Tiles for mixing
Gum arabic or gum tragacanth (any chemist)

Suitable underglaze colours:

2 oz. each of :
willow blue
blue green
citron yellow

jet black
brown
crimson red

Basic oxides:

Cobalt oxide
Copper oxide
Iron oxide

Manganese oxide
Lead antimoniate

Enamel or on-glaze colours
Liquid medium for colours
Genuine turpentine

Useful but not necessary

Banding wheel or turntable.

6. Firing and Glazing

WHAT HAPPENS TO A POT WHEN FIRED

DURING firing the nature of the clay is altered by chemical changes; it ceases to be clay and becomes pottery. Although clay may seem quite dry, when it is packed in a kiln it still contains some water. From 0° to 120°C. this 'water of formation' dries out and is replaced by air; between 350° and 500°C. chemically combined water is driven off, and by 900°C. organic matter has burnt away. At this point the most fusible ingredients of some clays will have begun to melt and bind together the more refractory ones. Some low grade clays will have 'matured', that is, reached the maximum temperature they can withstand without deformation. As the firing continues the melted matter flows into and fills up the pores of the pottery, until, if there is a sufficient proportion of refractory elements, vitrification takes place (see chapter 2). Maturing temperatures vary with individual clays.

This first firing turns earthenware clay into what is called 'biscuit', which is hard, dry and porous, but unless it is glazed it will not hold water and its porous surface will make it difficult to clean.

KILNS

Before long a potter will want to have control over the firing of his own pots, and a kiln will become a necessity. But until the beginner feels committed enough to invest in this rather expensive piece of equipment, the local possibilities for getting pots fired should be investigated. Some small commercial potteries will fire work for individuals, charging according to the height, weight or volume of the object. Sometimes an artist potter is willing to help and, certainly, every pottery class at an Art School or Institute will have facilities.

Choosing a kiln

Kilns are fired by electricity, gas, oil or solid fuel. Electric ones are the cleanest, the easiest to control and install, and would be the best choice for a beginner or anyone with limited space. Most manufacturers make a 3 kW. one with a muffle, that is the inside, measuring about 12 by 12 by 15 inches, which can be plugged into a normal domestic 13 or 15 amp. power plug. Bigger ones should be installed by an electrical contractor. A gas kiln has to have a chimney and a mains pipe, and is more difficult to control, though for an experienced potter, especially for stoneware, it allows more varied possibilities in firing. For anyone out of reach of mains services the most suitable type would probably be the one called 'an oil drip'. This is cheap to fire and easier to manipulate than a solid fuel one.

Electric, gas, oil drip or solid fuel kilns can be built at home, and some firms sell specifications and circuit diagrams. This is the cheapest way of getting one, and, if there are special needs, may be worthwhile.

FIRING

Primitive firing

There are one or two primitive ways of home firing which will be good enough for a low temperature biscuit. In one of these a simple brick kiln is built by laying bricks in the normal way, but without mortar, so that a hollow brick cube about three feet inside is formed; a brick is left out of the bottom course on each side as an air inlet. Four inches of sawdust is laid on the bottom and the first row of pots stacked upon it; after that the pots are covered in sawdust, and each layer of pottery is treated in the same way, finishing with a layer of sawdust on the top. If the top is lit with twigs the sawdust will burn downwards slowly, reaching, astonishingly enough, a temperature of about 850°C. A tin lid may be placed over the top during the firing, to aid the process. Since the sawdust is taking oxygen from the air, red clay turns almost black; in fact, if the pots are burnished beforehand with the back of a spoon, a very attractive finish will result. This kind of work cannot be glazed and the pottery is only useful for the storage of dry things, or as decoration.

Packing a biscuit kiln

To pack a kiln, batts or shelves and a number of props of varying heights are needed so that pots of varying heights can be packed safely and the whole height of the kiln used. The shelves will last longer if they are first painted with a thin mixture of flint or alumina and water (or a commercial batt wash) on the upper side. This will help to avoid the possibility of things sticking to them.

Put in the flattish things first on the floor of the kiln. Two or three pots can be stacked inside each other provided the weight is taken by the bases, but not the rims, and that heavy pots are not placed on more delicate work. Aim for a layer of approximately the same height and leave spaces for the props which must be high enough to support a shelf which clears the tallest pot. Each layer is packed in the same way, making sure that the props of each shelf stand directly above the ones below so that the weight is taken by the kiln floor. No pottery should touch the elements, but the kiln can be filled to capacity, as long as air can circulate everywhere. Pots covered with dark-toned slip occasionally affect others near by so they should be kept from touching anything or even be packed on a separate shelf.

Temperature gauge

It must be possible to check the temperature inside the kiln while firing, and the easiest way is to use a pyrometer which costs about £20. This has a meter connected to a rod inside the kiln, which registers degrees centigrade. Otherwise cones (little pyramids of a special ceramic mixture which melt and bend over at specific temperatures) are used. These are placed in the kiln in view of the spy hole. One which melts at the temperature required and one at twenty degrees lower are essential, and, until the potter can judge the approximate temperature of the kiln from the colour of the inside, it is advisable to include a cone melting at 800°C.

These cones must be fixed in their sockets, tipped slightly so that as they melt they will bend in the same direction and not interfere with each other. They must be arranged when packing the kiln so that they are visible from the spy hole; this can be checked by putting a piece of burning paper in the kiln and shutting the door. Some kilns have such tiny spy holes (in order to conserve heat) that it is impossible to see more than one cone, and these should be fitted with a pyrometer unless the potter has had great experience in firing.

FIRING All kilns have some sort of device for controlling the rate at which the temperature rises. If the gauge is marked 'low', 'medium' and 'high', then start on 'low'; but if it is calibrated from one to a hundred, then between 15 and 30 (the thicker the pots the lower the number). In order to let out evaporating moisture, leave the spy hole open, or remove the special bung if one is provided. It is most important that the initial part of the biscuit firing should be carried out with the gauge at 'low' (allow roughly three hours before turning to 'medium' for a small kiln) for too fierce a firing would damage the pottery. The spy hole or bung should not be closed until the temperature has reached 600°C. At 800°C. it can be switched to 'high' for the rest of the firing.

COOLING It would be fatal to the pots, and probably to the potter, to open up the kiln until it has cooled. The cooling must be gentle, as the pottery cannot stand the strain of a sudden change in temperature, so leave for twelve to twenty-four hours according to the size of the kiln.

FAULTS There may be certain difficulties in biscuit firing: pots may warp, bits may flake off, or cracks appear. In the case of flaking there may have been air in the clay; splitting can be caused by packing too many things on top of each other, warping because the object was too thin; perhaps the clay was not absolutely dry, or the firing too fast. Impatience over the length of time needed for firing is a common difficulty; heavy pots and especially any models which vary in thickness are likely to suffer the most if fired too quickly.

Packing a glaze kiln

Much more care must be taken when packing for a glaze firing, and there should be a gap the width of a finger between the pots so that they can touch neither each other nor the sides of the kiln. As previously suggested a thin layer of flint washed over the floor and shelves will help to absorb any glaze which might run off the pottery and will help to keep the kiln in good condition.

FIRING Glaze firing can be done much more quickly as no internal changes occur in the pot. Just switch on 'low' for the first half hour, leaving the bung out or spy hole open. Then turn to 'high' and replace the bung. Cool in the same way, but be very cautious if little pinging noises can be heard; this means that the glaze is tending to crack and the door must be shut for a little longer.

FAULTS Bad packing causes most of the damage likely to occur in glaze firing but the 'crazing' of glaze is another common difficulty. Fine cracks may appear in the glaze either immediately after firing or within the next few days or even months. It is often caused by the fact that the firing temperature of the biscuit was too low, and can sometimes be rectified by just refiring the pot at a higher temperature. Otherwise it is caused by the glaze contracting more than the body; this can sometimes be put right by adding flint to the glaze mixture. Peeling happens when the body shrinks more than the glaze, and is much harder to adjust. The best thing is to seek the advice of the supplier.

GLAZING

GLAZING earthenware amounts to covering the pot with a thin layer of glass and a second (glost) firing is required for it. A very simple description of the composition of glaze is that it is clay with added fluxes, usually some form of lead, borax or soda. The actual composition of glazes is very much more complex and there are countless varieties. The glaze must fit the body like a skin, so that as a pot cools after the glost firing both contract equally, thereby preventing crazing or peeling. To decide which glazes to use then, it is necessary either to study the whole chemistry of glazes and make many experiments, or to buy a few ready-mixed varieties from a supplier, who will have bodies and glazes that fit, and be willing to give advice should difficulties arise. A student who wishes to study this subject thoroughly, should, of course, start with the basic ingredients of glaze, mixing his own from recipes, and then developing them. But for a beginner working in his own home, possibly with little space for work or storage, it is advisable to choose the second way.

One colourless transparent glaze and one opaque white are the necessary minimum, and it is convenient to select those which mature at the same temperature. This range can be extended to include various forms of matt glaze. As experience is gained experiments can be made with these basic glazes until a more personal result is arrived at.

Transparent Glaze

Transparent glaze reveals the colour of the clay body and any decoration only slightly altered in colour and tone; it adds a little thickness and weight to the pot and gives it a smooth shiny surface like that of most of the crockery in everyday use. Most transparent glazes used today are leadless (except for various forms of modern fritted lead) because of the dangers of lead poisoning, but a mellow, slightly golden glaze which gave richness and unity to Early English slipware was obtained with a type of raw lead glaze which a few individual potters still use. Any transparent glaze may, however, be coloured by the addition of metal oxides with rich effects. The Persians, for example, covered their black-decorated vases with fine turquoise glaze; Edwardian tiled fireplaces, sometimes lifeless in design, are often rich in colour.

Majolica, Faience or Delft are the names given to ware covered with glaze containing tin oxide. This gives an opaque white glaze which does not 'run' in the firing. These qualities make it very suitable for rich painted decoration which is done on top of the unfired glaze. In the days when white porcelain ranked with precious metals as a material suitable for tableware and ornaments for the wealthy, most people ate from simple wooden plates or coarse brown pottery. By the sixteenth and seventeenth centuries, the middle classes wanted something better than the coarse ware but could not afford imported porcelain; this kind of glazed pottery, a substitute china, was introduced to meet the need.

PREPARATION Prepared glazes can be obtained as a white powder which only has to be mixed with water and sieved through a 100 mesh sieve before use. The correct consistency for glaze is roughly that of thin cream, but it varies according to the absorbency of the biscuit. The higher the biscuit-firing temperature the less porous the body will be, and, as a consequence, the glaze must be thicker. A rough test for glaze consistency is that it must not run off the pot leaving bare patches, nor must it be so thick that it cracks. Tin glazes are thicker than other types.

STORAGE Mixed glaze can be kept indefinitely in a jar or canister with a lid, as this will stop the water evaporating and dust from falling into it. Some of the particles of glaze are heavy and do not stay in suspension for long, so it is wise to keep it well stirred both before and during use. If at any time the glaze does become lumpy it should be passed through a 100 mesh sieve.

Coloured glaze

Mention has been made of coloured glazes and these are easy to make and interesting to use. The same oxides are used as those for colouring slip: cobalt – blue, copper – green, manganese – purply brown. Underglaze colours, especially made glaze tints, or ready-made coloured glazes can also be used. (See Appendix.)

PREPARATION Most oxides need no special sieving, but cobalt is inclined to speckle so pass it through a 200 mesh sieve. The colouring and glaze must be thoroughly mixed, and this is best done by sieving through a 100 mesh sieve. Experiments will have to be made with different proportions, starting with something like a dessertspoonful of powdered colouring to one pint of liquid glaze. The more oxide, the stronger the colour, but each has its own idiosyncracies: copper, for instance, will produce a kind of metallic pewter effect if too much is added, but this has attractions and can be exploited. Manganese, more than the other oxides, makes the glaze flux at a lower temperature and it may therefore run a little, but, if it is dabbed on top of a glaze, a streaky effect can be achieved; cobalt, again, is hard to mix unless really ground hard with a pestle and mortar but the speckle it creates is quite individual. The oxides, as with slip, may be mixed to produce other colours.

There are, indeed, many possibilities, and your own work will suggest further experiment; in fact, for some potters glazing becomes their main interest in surface treatment.

A few of the pots illustrated have interesting glazes, though black and white reproductions do not do them justice. The pot on plate 28 has a dark blue speckle in a green glaze which is in keeping with the simplicity of the pot, the whole having an almost pebble-like quality. Plate 30 shows a crazed glaze giving another sort of surface treatment; plate 36 an example of a thick white glaze used to contrast with unglazed areas. Plate 3 shows a lively pair of pots on which a white tin glaze has been run over a black. Plate 34 is an example where more control has been exercised in the running together of coloured glazes.

Application

A pot can be glazed by dipping, pouring or spraying. The aim is the same – to get a thin even coat over the whole.

Spraying is easier with an electric paint spray. In its absence an insecticide spray, garden, hair-lacquer, scent or any other kind of spray may be tried; any one may be successful if it is powerful enough, has a fine enough nozzle, and, if in the effort of using it, the direction and the distance from the pot can be controlled. A plastic diffuser bottle (9d. or 1s. in a hardware shop) can, with practice, be used, though it is not so good for large objects.

The time-honoured methods of dipping and pouring require considerably more skill, but they are well worth practising. These ways are not only much quicker (when mastered) but they produce a glaze layer whose varying thickness is directly related to the shape of the pot, whilst the sprayed glaze has either a mechanical evenness or an arbitrary blotchiness. Also the dipped or poured glaze adheres more closely to the pot and is less likely to be damaged in handling.

POURING METHOD To glaze the insides of pots and the outsides of large ones it is best to pour the glaze. Have ready plenty of glaze in a jug, and a clean bowl. For the inside fill the pot three-quarters full of glaze and quickly empty it out into the bowl, turning the pot at the same time so that the whole surface is covered. A sharp, shaking movement will help to remove any surplus which may otherwise dry in lumps on the lip. To glaze the outside the pot is held upside down and the glaze poured over it. The pot must be manipulated so that awkward surfaces such as the undersides of handles are not left uncovered.

DIPPING After the glaze on the inside has dried, the outside may be covered by dipping it. Put one hand inside the pot, holding it by pressing outwards against the sides with the fingers and thumb, and insert the pot base downwards into the glaze. It must be kept level so that no glaze runs over the rim into the inside. There must be sufficient glaze to reach the top of the pot, held in a bucket large enough to accommodate both pot and glaze. Alternatively hold the pot by its base and dip it rim end first, air pressure will prevent the inside from being glazed a second time. Open shaped dishes can be glazed in one process by passing them through glaze in one steady motion.

Wherever the pot has been held bare patches will be left, which must be covered with glaze brushed on with a soft brush. Care should be taken to hold the pot where finger marks will be inconspicuous.

DIFFICULTIES If for any reason lumps of thick glaze form, leave them until they have completely dried out; for then it is possible to remove a little of the worst bumps by gently scraping with a sharp blade or rubbing with the fingers; transparent glaze does flow just enough in the firing to even out slight bumps but tin glaze is not so obliging. Should the whole operation go wrong, wash everything off under the tap, let the pot thoroughly dry out, and repeat the process. Any painted decoration under the glaze will have to be done again.

Difficulty in making the glaze stay on at all means either that the glaze is too thin or the pot has been over fired. In the second case try warming the pot before glazing. A good way of testing the amount of absorbency to expect from a pot is to put your tongue on it; you will soon learn from the intensity of what is known as 'plucking' just how hard the biscuit is.

Preparation for firing

Once the glaze is on satisfactorily it must be absolutely dry before being fired. It will become quite white and chalky and will easily rub off, so it must be handled carefully. Since the glaze actually melts during the firing, any part of it which touches the kiln will stick fast, and it is very important to wipe the foot completely clear of glaze. Otherwise set the pot on a stilt when packing the kiln, the stilt being a special fireclay stand which supports the pot on three fine points which only leave tiny marks. If you are not firing your own kiln do not rely on this method being used, for it is a tricky business to arrange properly and commercial potteries can rarely spare the time.

Fault

One further common trouble is 'crawling'; this is when the glaze has run off in places, leaving bare patches. It can be caused by grease or dust on the biscuit, or by the fact that the glaze was too thickly applied or not allowed to dry thoroughly.

Once involved in pottery making, it is essential to have a small kiln; so many experiments and individual discoveries can be made. One has to have opened the kiln door after a glaze firing to know just how thrilling an experience it is. Indeed much of the skill and excitement of pottery-making is involved in the firing.

'The few hours before opening the kiln door I get very excited, but when the kiln doors are opened I always feel disappointed and become depressed for a few days. I sometimes am glad that I made a certain piece but at the time I am incapable of judging where I have failed or succeeded; somehow in my mind I see them in a nebulous perfection. When the kiln door is open there is the reality – everything looks so solid and meagre. The funny thing is that no matter how many kilns I have opened it hasn't cured me of this dream. I still have this misty apparition of nebulous perfection and am still chasing after it'.*

*Pottery Quarterly No. 29, 'Ways of Working and Thinking', by Brian Newman.

Materials and equipment

2 to 5 lb. of leadless transparent glaze
2 to 5 lb. of leadless opaque white, or tin glaze
100 mesh sieve. (Same as chapter 4)
Metal oxides for colouring or glaze stains

Useful but not necessary

Glaze spray
Kiln
Kiln furniture:

Shelves	Stilts
Props	Flint
Cones or Pyrometer	

7. Thrown Pottery

IT must be said at the outset that for this sort of work there is no substitute for a first-class teacher. This is why this important part of pottery making has been left so late – because it involves a real commitment to the craft, requiring a wheel, a special place to work, and constant practice before even modest results may be achieved. Many amateurs have gained great skill, and through it satisfaction, by joining the classes offered by many local authorities.

Because a teacher is so necessary we do not claim that the outline in this chapter is sufficient to give the reader all the knowledge, practical and aesthetic, to throw well; we hope that the description is sufficient to acquaint those who are determined to be potters with something of what they are in for, and enough to help those who are not going to throw towards a better understanding of the different qualities of work they may encounter. This way of making pottery is most rewarding, and the pottery produced very lively, subtle and full of character.

THROWING

All thrown pottery, except for plates, saucers or shallow bowls, is developed from a cylinder that is often referred to as the basic cylinder; to make this a series of distinctly different hand actions must be performed, each of which has to be learnt individually, and these may vary considerably as each potter develops his own method. The following is only one of several techniques.

To make the basic cylinder

Throw a ball of well-wedged clay as near as possible on to the centre of the wheel head, pat it into a cone shape, wet both hands and the clay, and make the wheel revolve fast (plate *j*). The hands must be kept wet during the whole process to prevent them sticking to the clay. Containing the whole mass within the hands, squeeze the clay until it works up into a cone (plate *k*), and then press down again to a compact lump (plate *l*), finally centring it with a steady hand (plate *m*). The clay should now be a symmetrical mass, concentric with the wheel. This is perhaps the most difficult operation of all. It is essential to keep the hands steady and it may be necessary to rest the left arm on the tray with the elbow against the hip. To keep the clay centred avoid any sudden, jerky movements. After centring but still holding the clay with the left hand, make a hole in the centre with the right thumb, steadying the right hand by resting the fingers on those of the left hand; the result will be a thick, squat pot (plate *n*). The next move is to squeeze the thick wall between the thumb and first finger so that it thins and rises a little; the rim is made even by holding it, as it spins, in the crutch between thumb and first finger (plate *o*). After this, put the left hand inside the pot, keeping the elbow in the air, and, gathering the clay from the base between the fingers of the left hand on the inside and the crooked first finger of the right hand on the outside, squeeze gently, move the hands upwards behind the bulk of the clay as it rises, being careful not to force the movement: the pot will rise in spectacular fashion. This movement is repeated until a fairly thick-walled cylinder is formed (plate *p*).

Shaping

Any shaping from the basic cylinder is done now. Start right from the base, squeezing with both hands in the same position as before. If an outward curve is to be made allow the inside hand to overtake the outside one and use more pressure on the inside: to return the curve the opposite is done, that is, the outside hand overtakes the one inside. To narrow the cylinder, a method known as collaring can be used, in which the clay is gradually coaxed by means of a throttling movement, into giving the cylinder a smaller neck (plate q). This is quite difficult to do without causing a diagonal ripple which often results in the pot collapsing. Certain details have now to be finished – the rim and base must be trimmed (plates r and s) and the water mopped out of the inside with a sponge – after which the wheel is stopped.

If the rim of the pot becomes uneven trim it level; half a needle, the broken end of which has been stuck into a cork, makes the best instrument for this. While the wheel revolves, steady the inside of the rim of the pot with the forefinger of the left hand, and, keeping the needle level, press it through from the outside until it makes contact with the forefinger, and lift off the surplus ring of clay. The resulting sharp edge should be rounded off with a sponge or the finger tips.

Cutting off

To cut the pot off the wheel take a fine wire, preferably twisted, and, stretching it taut across the wheel head with the thumbs holding it down, drag it under the pot (plate t). Put some water on the wheel and keep dragging the wire through until it has pulled enough water under the pot to allow it to slide easily. Then, either pick it up with both hands and quickly place it on the board, or slide it on to a wet hand held level with the wheel head and then on to a wet board. Once on the board it must be left to dry out to the 'leather hard' stage.

Throwing open shapes

Flat bowls and plates are made with a wide base of solid clay, as otherwise they might collapse; only the inside shape is actually thrown, the outside being formed afterwards by turning (see next paragraph). The heel of the hand can be used instead of the thumb for opening a large piece of clay. As wide shapes are difficult to remove from the wheel without distortion occurring they are often thrown on batts secured to the wheelhead with pieces of sticky clay.

TURNING

This name is given to the process of trimming a thrown pot at the leather hard stage in order to refine the shape at the base, to give it a foot ring by hollowing the underside, or occasionally to decorate it with horizontal grooves.

To turn, the pot is inverted on the centre of the wheel. To test that it is exactly centred, hold a sharp point (the point of a turning tool or hat pin) just clear of the surface of the pot and rotate the wheel slowly; if the pot is not centred the point will make a horizontal scratch along part of the circumference. Stop the wheel, find the part of the scratch which is deepest, and push the pot away from this point across the centre of the wheel head. Continue to adjust in this way until it is running true. The pot is then fixed in position with a roll of clay which touches the rim all round and is firmly pressed to the wheel head.

The tools needed for turning can be made from strips of steel about an ⅛″ thick (see plates *u*, *v*, *w*) or they can be bought from a supplier. Holding the tool firmly in the right hand and steadying it with the left, let the wheel rotate fairly briskly. First flatten the base, working from the middle outwards (plate *u*), then trim the wall of the pot (plate *v*). In the case of open shapes a good deal of surplus clay will need to be cut away. Last of all, shape the foot; this means cutting down all but the rim of the base so as to leave a raised ring on which the pot will stand steadily (plate w). The shape of the foot and the way in which the outside profile of the pot meets it are matters of individual taste. A study of the illustrations through the book will serve to show how the treatment of the foot ring has been varied.

There is some disagreement between potters about the desirability of turning, especially of touching the outer profile. The argument runs that the character of a thrown shape is quite different from that of a turned one, and, therefore, that the life and line of the shape will be spoilt. Be that as it may, the difference must be recognized: turning certainly gives a mechanical character to a shape. Either limit turning as much as possible or turn the whole profile.

CHATTER If a rippled surface begins to develop try holding the point of a triangular tool directly at the surface of the pot so that fine scoring marks are made, and then remove them by turning. This 'chatter', as it is called, can be caused by blunt tools, tools held at the wrong angle, or by the potter's hands not being steady. It can also be started off by the presence of foreign bodies or knots of hard clay due to faulty wedging.

To keep the hands steady, rest the right arm on the edge of the wheel, whenever possible steadying the right hand with the left. And remember to breathe.

WHEELS

In the selection of a wheel there are several points to be considered. Kick wheels are cheaper than electric ones – from £30 to £40 as against £75 to £90. Other factors to consider are these: there is a much finer control of speed with a kick wheel (very important for turning), but the action involved requires quite a lot of energy, making it difficult to have absolutely steady hands, especially at high speeds. The electric type, being powered, makes for easier centring and speeds up the throwing process, though generally the slowest speed is often too fast for turning, especially for tall pots.

When the type has been decided, look more closely into the design from the point of view of ease of cleaning, whether there is a seat, and, if there is, how it adjusts. Make sure the speed control of a power wheel is well placed, and that the action of the foot bar on a kick wheel suits you (side or forward kick).

Most well-known suppliers sell wheels, and their catalogues are very informative. Occasionally potteries are sold up and equipment may be bought second-hand. *Pottery Quarterly* and other craft magazines have advertisements in most issues.

*

It is more difficult to discuss the basic form of pottery than its decoration; when one starts to decorate there is at least a shape ready, something to relate to. There are, however, a few basic rules which generally apply.

A pot is unlikely to be satisfactory if it is made symmetrical about its horizontal axis as it will appear to have no definite top and bottom; a pot with a totally concave profile will sometimes appear to have too much accent on its extremities and be weak in the middle; a pot should never be made up of two equal volumes – (imagine the collar of the jug on plate 9 to be half as high again) – as duality will result; a pot whose contour consists of a concave and convex profile of equal length may not appear unified; and so on.

But these are all negative strictures mainly to do with the avoidance of very bad form rather than positive encouragements in the direction of subtle form. It is important to study examples of good pottery, and the following criticism of the forms selected for illustration may be helpful.

The Kwantung vase (plate 28) is the simplest form in the book – no base, rim, handles or decoration. Had it been symmetrical about its horizontal axis it would have been very dull: as it is, the form, weighted towards the top, gives great satisfaction. Of all the pots illustrated, it is perhaps the most monumental, the one which looks as though it will last for ever.

The example on plate 32 dangerously approaches symmetry about a horizontal axis: in this case it is the decoration and attachments which weight this pot satisfactorily – the dark base, the rings asymmetrically placed, the neck and handles. It has, of course, a quite different character from the former example, equally sophisticated, but less aloof.

The vase on plate 28 already referred to, with its larger diameter nearer the top, is quite satisfactory without a rim, and, indeed, the tall pot on plate 31 could be imagined without one. This is not usually so with a pot whose largest diameter is towards the bottom: it is formally necessary then, in order to redress the balance, either to make use of a counter curve, to use a rim as in the delightfully decorated Korean vase (plate 29), or to be positive with handles (see the subtle handles of the pot on plate 30 and their close-up on plate 39, which provide detailed complexity against the extreme simplicity of the shape).

The classical Greek pot on plate 15 shows a different way of successfully concluding a shape whose largest diameter is nearer the top, that is by allowing the form to haunch up to a wide shoulder and setting a quite positive neck and rim upon it: the danger lies in the neck becoming too dominant.

The three jugs shown on plates 9, 10 and 44 make an interesting study. The first one is perfect in its proportions (see the section on Carved Decoration in chapter 4), the plain base and straight collar being exactly the right foil to the swelling, decorated part. The English jug (plate 10) is lively and charming, but not quite right: the concave and convex curves are about equal in length and the handle unfortunately breaks the continuity of the ring. The industrially made but hand-painted jug (plate 44) is delightful; the well-shaped lid, handle and spout all sit in balance to complete a satisfying composition.

There are, occasionally, pots which fascinate because of their dramatic originality. The Chinese Amphora (plate 38) is such a one. Instead of the handles being minor attachments they are part of the main form: the pot gives the impression of having been made by carving out two holes so as to form the body and handles – though, of course, it was not made in this way.

Plate 36 shows a modern pot, which, though much quieter, has a certain uniqueness about it. It is difficult to find modern examples whose derivations are not immediately obvious, examples where the original style has been transmuted into something more authentically individual. This pot has its own personality.

Plate 34 also shows some work with a personal stamp. Though it is difficult to capture its quality in a photograph, there is an unusual delight in moving it in the hands to see its form; both pots are almost elliptical in plan and are made by throwing in the normal way, slitting the bottom, and then pressing the pot together in the hands.

Although these pots illustrate a great variety of shapes, and while it is desirable to experiment as much as possible, it is well to remember that many potters work for long periods on variations of one shape so that the theme is thoroughly explored.

1. Hand-built Japanese
tea bowl

2. Coiled pot 18 in. high

3. Coiled pots

4. Twentieth-century coiled pot by Ladi-Kwali 14 in. high

5. Slab pot 13 in. high

6. (*below*) Slab pots by P. Brown and A. Wallwork 6 to 7 in. high

7. Pressed dishes
showing slip-trailed
decoration

8. (*above*) Hand-built
Aztec pot showing
carved decoration
9¼ in. high

9. (*top right*) Thrown
Persian jug showing
carved decoration
6¼ in. high

10. (*right*) Thrown
Staffordshire jug with
sgraffito decoration
9½ in. high

11. (*top left*) Thrown
bread bin with raised
decoration by G. Naylor
15½ in. high

12. (*left*) Thrown
storage jars by P. Wright
2½ to 3½ in. high

13. (*above*) Thrown
dishes by W. Norland

14. Nineteenth-century cast jug 7½ in. high

15. Painted Greek Hydria 20 in. high

18. (*right*) Twentieth-century dish with slip-trailed decoration 10 in. in diameter (Amateur)

16. Seventeenth-century
dish with sgraffito decoration
11½ in. high

17. Eighteenth-century dish
showing slip-trailed decoration
17¼ in. high

19. Persian thirteenth-century dish 7¾ in. in diameter

20. Twentieth-century Spanish dish 12 in. in diameter

21. Sixteenth-century Spanish dish 16 in. in diameter

22. Seventeenth-century Lambeth dish 13¼ in. in diameter

23. Greek mixing bowl 10½ in. in diameter

24. (*below*) Plaque by S. Irwin

25. (*right*) Detail of brushwork of plate 32

26. (*below right*) Detail of brushwork of plate 20

27. Detail of brushwork
of plate 22

28. Kwantung vase
10½ in. high

29. Korean vase

30. Sung jar 6½ in. high

31. Sung vase 18 in. high

32 (*right*) Sung vase

33. Stoneware pot by
P. Barron 15 in. high

34. Stoneware bottles
by P. Barron 5½ to
9 in. high

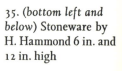

35. (*bottom left and
below*) Stoneware by
H. Hammond 6 in. and
12 in. high

36. Stoneware pot by J. Kidman

37. Neolithic Chinese pot 15½ in. high

38. Chinese Amphora

39. (*below*) Detail of handles of plate 30

40. (*top left opposite*) Eighteenth-century Virgin and Child 8¼ in. high

41. (*top right opposite*) Eighteenth-century modelled figures

42. (*below opposite*) Cat by M. Lambert and fish by S. Irwin

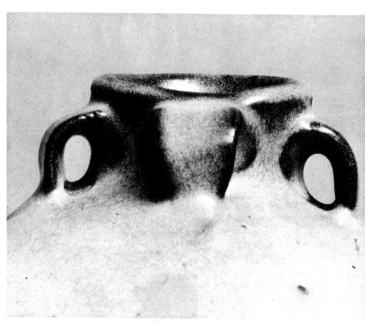

43. Chinese guarding lion

44. Eighteenth-century milk jug 5½ in. high

45. Cast vase by R. Mitchell

46. Domestic pottery

Isaac Button, a traditional, non-art school potter in Yorkshire, who still makes by hand large amounts of useful and beautiful pottery for sale, when asked about David Leach and his students with repetitive throwing, twinkled in approval: 'Master one shape and the rest will follow more readily.'*

Essential equipment

Throwing wheel	Small natural sponge
Fine cutting wire	Large sponge for cleaning wheel
Boards	A triangular turning tool
Bowl for water	1 square turning tool
Needle in a cork	

*Pottery Quarterly, No. 29, 'Ways of Working and Thinking', by Brian Newman.

8. *Attachments*

JUGS, mugs, canisters, teapots have additions in the way of handles, spouts, lips or lids without which they cannot serve their proper purposes. These later additions should be kept in mind from the beginning; it is no use, for example, trying to fit a good-looking, functional lip to a shape which splays out at the top. Many a well-shaped pot has been spoiled by ill-shaped handles, or by handles which, although good in themselves, relate awkwardly to the pot.

MAKING A HANDLE

Handles for hand-thrown pots are usually made by 'pulling'. A piece of well-wedged clay is first rolled into a carrot shape. Grip this at the top with one hand, wet the other one, hold the thumb and forefinger in such a way that the clay is in the fork between them, and gently squeeze the clay, pulling downwards from the gripping hand to the bottom. This action should be repeated, always keeping the pulling hand wet and making sure that the clay is hanging vertically, until a slightly tapering length of clay is made whose section is elliptical (plate x). To keep the section even, continually turn the clay in the gripping hand. It may be modified by setting the position of the finger and thumb differently for the last few movements. A common mistake is to make the section too round; it should be nearer a strap than a tube shape.

At the first attempt the end of the handle may be pulled off, and the whole may be lumpy instead of tapering smoothly. To guard against this, have only well-wedged clay, use plenty of water so the hand does not stick to the clay, and keep an even and gentle pressure when pulling.

When two or three successful lengths have been achieved, press the thick ends on to a board, letting the rest hang over, thereby setting the spring of the handle. They must dry until they are stiff enough to retain their shape, but not so hard that they crack if they are bent. Should they be too soft, lay on a plaster batt to dry off a little before allowing them to hang.

Fixing the handle

Cut the handle carefully from the stub at an angle suitable for the pot to which it will be fixed. Before sticking it, gently bend the handle to the approximate shape intended, hold it against the pot with the profile at eye level, and decide the place from which the top should spring. After scoring the pot fix in the usual way, using slurry. The inside is supported with one hand and the two surfaces are pressed well together (plate *y*). Check the shape of the handle again and decide the place for the lower attachment, making sure it is vertically below the upper one; also check that the whole handle is springing at right angles to the surface, by looking down at it, planwise. Fix the bottom in the same way as the top.

A soft handle with a large curve near the top will some-times sag, so leave the pot upside down until it is set. Should it crack or pull away from the pot repairs can sometimes be done by pressing a coil of clay into the angle between handle and pot and working it in with a wooden tool.

The size of handle must be considered in relation to the weight of the pot and its use. A pint tankard needs a handle big enough to take three masculine fingers, for instance. Remember, too, in determining size, that the handle will shrink more than the pot as it is slightly wetter when attached.

MAKING A LIP

In addition to a handle a jug must have a lip and a teapot a spout. The easiest way to form a lip is to pull it from the jug as soon as this has been thrown. With fingers wet, place the first two of one hand slightly apart on the outside of the rim, put the first finger of the other hand between them with the tip inside, and gently pull outwards, at the same time holding the rim back firmly with the other hand (plate z). If, in spite of this, the top of the jug should distort, run a wet finger round the inside to reshape it.

Lips may be made separately. Throw a small bowl the shape of which is dictated by the profile of the required lip. While still soft squeeze a section of the curve of the bowl at the rim. When it has set the section is cut off, trimmed to fit the pot exactly, and attached with slurry. The inside wall can be cut away entirely or perforated.

MAKING A SPOUT

To make a spout a cone or bottle shape is thrown: its precise form will be determined by the shape of the pot and the necessity for harmony between it and the spout. When it is 'leather hard' cut the wide end diagonally at the desired angle and trim until it fits the curve of the pot. The narrow end is also trimmed to an angle suitable for pouring. The area of pot to be covered is perforated, the line of attachment scored, rubbed with slurry, and the spout fixed. Make sure the lip of the spout is at least as high as the top of the pot to avoid an overflow when it is filled (see figures 19 and 20).

MAKING LIDS

If the pots have been made by the 'coiling' or 'slab' methods, their lids must be made in the same way. A lid for a thrown

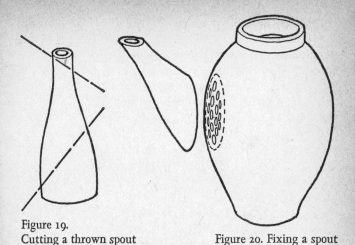

Figure 19.
Cutting a thrown spout

Figure 20. Fixing a spout

pot must be made at the same time and from the same clay as
the pot, to ensure a good fit. Throw the shape upside down,

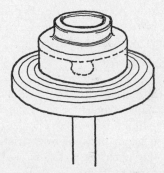

Figure 21. Turning a lid

leaving a base sufficiently thick to allow for a knob to be
turned later (figure 21). Alternatively the knob can be thrown
separately or modelled by hand and attached after the lid has
been turned.

There are different types of lids (figure 22). Care should be taken to choose one suitable for the function of the pot; for instance, a teapot must have a lid which will stay on when tilted for pouring.

These ways of making attachments are the standard ones,

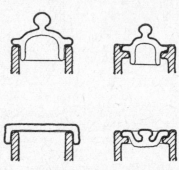

Figure 22. Types of lid

but there are many variations – for example, handles may be made of plaited or twisted coils, knobs can be modelled in the form of fruit and flowers and so on.

*

The attachments described may be shaped in different ways: a handle, for example, may have a single curve as in plate 44, a curve and straight line (plate 9) or a double curve (plate 10). Limited to these shapes only, a great variation of profile is possible, depending upon the precise form of the curve, the relationship of curve to straight, or, in the last case, the contrast of convex and concave curve. In any pot, the way in which the handle relates to the main shape is most important, but the junction of handle to pot is also crucial.

Look at the form of the handle shown on plate 44 – a sharp upward loop at the top which slows down to a gradual curve at the bottom. The underside of the handle at the top is smoothed into the profile of the jug (a very common method) while the lower end comes in at a fairly wide angle. A common mistake is to bring the lower end in at too narrow an angle, and if this is done it is essential to round in the top edge to the profile by tooling in a small coil of clay.

It is interesting to speculate whether this handle could have been better designed. Should the top end approach at a near right angle, connecting with the painted band? If so, then both junctions would be too similar, and a counter curve joined in a scroll at the bottom would perhaps be necessary. But this, surely, would be too flamboyant for the otherwise placid curves of this pot. Alternatively, should the underside of the lower junction have been smoothed in? And would the top side of the same junction have been better rounded upwards? Every handle can be a tantalizing problem.

The handle of the pot shown on plate 9 stubs almost vertically into the shoulder. This is, of course, only possible, when there is a narrow collar on a wide-bellied pot.

The pot shown on plate 10 has a satisfactory handle with a double curve, the lower junction of which corresponds with a decorative band (plates 15 and 23 show that this has been a practice in different periods). It also illustrates a common way of completing the top of a decorated jug – by treating the rim and lips as one. This probably derived from an earlier practice of using pewter or silver for finishing lips and rims, presumably to prevent chipping.

Plates 15 and 23 illustrate a loop type handle attached horizontally. The bread crock (plate 11) has side lugs as well as a strong handle to the lid which happily completes the overall design.

The importance of the relationship between handle and pot is most dramatically illustrated in the example of the Chinese

Amphora (plate 38). In a different way the small, loop handles on the Sung pot (plate 39) are equally significant in the composition of the whole.

Essential equipment

Boards
Ruler
Sponge

9. Modelling

THE sculptor has always used clay for both large- and small-scale work. It is the material with which he can build up forms from the inside, instead of cutting away from the block as he would in the case of wood or stone. In fact, the sculptor wishing to model a standing figure, for example, makes a metal skeleton called an armature on which he superimposes his clay; this is a practical necessity as it holds the clay together as the bones hold the flesh. It is a method which makes possible statues of rearing horses and delicately poised ballet dancers, or spiky, abstract forms. But unfired clay is not a permanent material, so that this sort of work is finally cast in another material, usually bronze or plaster. The other alternative is to fire the clay, but here other problems arise; an armature, no impediment to casting, makes firing impossible, and if the work is very large in scale it is unlikely that a kiln will hold it.

There is, however, a range of small-scale sculpture in clay known as terracotta. Much is possible in this field as long as the work is self-supporting, is not too large, and is fired with care. It is, still, more in the province of the sculptor than the potter, produced by his modelling methods rather than by the specific pottery processes we have been dealing with.

A third, particular type of modelling with clay which we will call 'pottery modelling', is even more specialized, and the same tools and techniques are employed as in pottery; the forms derive especially from its processes – rolling, coiling, moulding, decorating, glazing and so on. Like terracotta work, it must be self-supporting, which is why so many ceramic figure groups have strange tree stumps connecting with unlikely parts of the anatomy, or convenient draperies filling in gaps between limbs, strengthening the lower part of the model; sitting or reclining poses are often chosen.

A pottery model must be made hollow or it will break up in the firing. There are several ways of doing this. One is to scoop out the clay in the centre from the base upwards, if necessary cutting the model into suitably sized pieces, hollowing them separately, and then sticking them together again with slurry. A second is to use the normal processes of coiling or throwing for the basic shapes, and then add solid pieces, or further coils. This compels the formalization proper to pottery. A third way is to make an original model from solid clay, and from this a mould which can be used to make as many hollow slip casts as are desired. This is of use only when several copies of the same model are required, and is an industrial method employed for mass production.

To make full use of his resources, a potter may use colour and glaze, and he must make the surface texture of his model suitable for them; in some cases features may be best painted rather than modelled – perhaps the mane of a horse or the face of a figure. The stylization of painting as well as of the shape itself gives to ceramic modelling a very special character, quite different from the work of a sculptor. The potter is bound by his craft and the kind of forms that are the result of its processes, but he delights in his craft, too; his work, by comparison, will be smaller in scale, probably more decorative and delicate in detail and lighter in mood.

MODELLING A FIGURE

Let us suppose that a figure of a woman holding a child is to be modelled, the whole composition to be about a foot high, and that it is to be decorated and glazed. It is most important in deciding the pose of the woman to remember that if she stands with nothing but her legs to support her body she will sag or collapse. She may have to sit, kneel, wear a long skirt, be standing in long grass or even have another child pushing against her – any convincing contrivance. The design should be compact, for anything like a pointing arm for example, is likely to droop or fall off.

Having wedged the clay, start to build up the main shapes with solid lumps well pressed together to avoid trapping air. At this stage forget about detail (too early a consideration of detail can be a snare in any medium), and concentrate on the main masses, the proportion, and the movements in the body; turn the head, twist the shoulders, bend the hip until the woman looks as though she is naturally bearing the weight of the child – experiment with variations until the most convincing pose is found. After this stage it will probably be better to let the clay dry a little so that it is firmer to work on, but do make sure that the added clay is pressed well in, with slip if necessary. The surface of the clay may be wholly smooth or textured, or a combination of both. The texture may be that caused naturally by the fingers building up the clay or it may be deliberately tooled to suggest hair, coarse cloth, and so on. As the finished model will probably be glazed it is better to aim for simple forms without too much naturalistic texture or sharp detail.

Hollowing out

When the model is finished, free it from the base board and allow it to become quite firm before hollowing it out. This is done from the bottom by scooping out the centre of the clay with a wire loop tool so that no more than ¾" thickness of clay wall is left. It may prove difficult to hollow the whole model from the bottom, in which case it must be cut in two, somewhere round the waistline, with a fine wire cutter, the remainder of the clay must be scooped from the top half, so that there are no separately enclosed hollow spaces within the model, and stuck together again with a little slurry. It is probable that some tidying up will be needed round the joint.

Firing, glazing and decorating are the same as for any pot, though a slow biscuit firing is even more important, for, because the walls of the model will not be exactly of even thickness, there will be greater strains under heat.

A delightful eighteenth-century composition of Virgin and Child is illustrated on plate 40. The design is compact and graceful and is well formalized, though the dark nipples of the baby detract somewhat from the eyes of the mother. Although it was, in fact, cast from a two-piece mould, it is the sort of work possible by direct modelling, though in this case a deeper relief would be possible.

POTTERY METHODS FOR MODELLING

All the methods already described for making pots can be used for models. Figures, animals or abstract forms may be built up with coils which can be left to reveal themselves completely, partially or not at all. Bent sheets of clay used either on their own or in conjunction with coils or slightly more solid modelling as in the lion (plate 43) are another way. If thrown shapes are the starting point they may be squashed, pinched, bent, cut in pieces, or stuck together. All these methods call for imagination and inventiveness and can result in work which is charming and light-hearted in character.

Plate 41 shows good examples of work done by eighteenth-century pottery modellers. The main shapes of the horse and his gentleman rider have been slip cast from a mould, the coat, reins, etc. made from flat pieces, the hair from small coils, the mane and tail indented. The basic shape of the lady, or rather of the clothed form of the lady, was thrown and turned, the arms made from rolls of clay, the cap from flat strips.

The examples on plate 42 are recent work, a plump fish (see indented decoration) and a lean cat which as well as being a fine model has been painted with skilful brushwork.

When in the late seventeenth-century the well-known English and Continental factories began to develop, a different process of slip casting was used for reproducing numbers of models from the same mould. Most of the pieces in museums were produced in this way – the highly refined Meissen porcelain, the popular Staffordshire figures, the models from the Copenhagen factory, Royal Doulton, Wedgwood, Rosenthal and many others.

Modelling for this kind of work is dependent upon the crafts of mould-making and slip-casting, and is dealt with in the next chapter.

10. Mould Making and Slip Casting

SLIP casting is a method widely used in industry for making domestic ware and reproducing models. It was evolved especially for the mass production of large quantities of identical pots made quickly by workers, each of whom was skilled at only one small part of the whole process.

The making of the actual mould from which the casts are taken is a very specialized craft. Nevertheless it is possible for a beginner to make simple ones.

The one-piece moulds for pressed dishes described in chapter 3 had to be designed without undercuts so that the clay could be removed undamaged, and this restricted their use to the making of open shapes. Moulds consisting of two or more pieces overcome this limitation and allow any form to be reproduced. The pieces of this mould are so made that when they are put together they form an apparently solid block of plaster which, in fact, contains the shape in negative – that is, a cavity which when filled with slip will produce a cast of the form desired. In order to pour the slip into the block a channel is made between the outside and this cavity.

Numerous casts can be made from these moulds which are filled with slip. The plaster absorbs some of the water until a crust begins to form, after which the rest of the liquid slip is poured out. The remaining crust is left to dry and a hollow replica of the original is left.

It is possible to make moulds from complex shapes, and some of the fine eighteenth-century porcelain groups, for example, necessitated a mould made in very many pieces. The eighteenth-century figures of contemporary celebrities, lovers, animals, etc., like the Salt glaze group on plate 40, are good examples of work done specifically for simple, two-piece moulds. The mother and child has no deep clefts or holes piercing the mass of the group: the figures are designed so that no form turns back on itself to make an undercut which would require that part to have a separate piece of mould. One piece of mould has covered the front of the group, ending on a line which forms the silhouette of the figure on this particular photograph: the other piece would have formed the back.

MODELLING FOR SLIP CASTING

When designing for this process the problem is to make a model with as few undercuts as possible so that the mould can consist of the minimum number of pieces. The clay of the cast shrinks as it dries and this allows for undercuts up to about $\frac{1}{8}''$ which, on a small figure for instance, is all that is needed for any details of features or drapery. The actual model is eventually scrapped, so that the clay used need not be wedged nor need any special care be taken in building it up.

Deciding the divisions of the mould

The easiest way of describing how to decide upon the lines of division of the pieces of the mould would be to demonstrate on an actual three dimensional piece. Since this is impossible, let us imagine that one is going to make a mould of a head. (See figures 23, 24, 25.) It will suffice to show the kind of problems encountered with most models. Try to imagine the mould being made in two pieces divided on a line running up the middle of the back of the neck and head, over the top, down the centre of the forehead, nose, chin and neck; this, of course, will not cope with the ears which would be

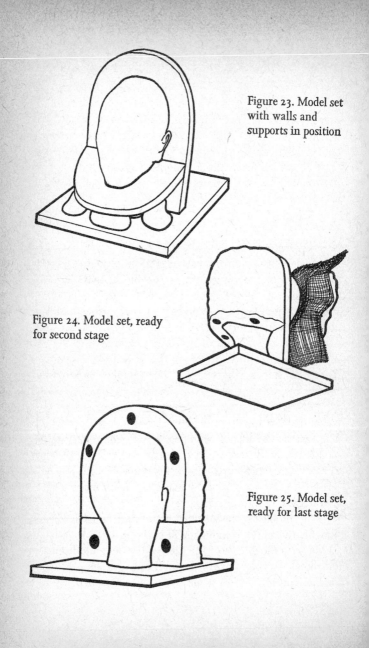

Figure 23. Model set with walls and supports in position

Figure 24. Model set, ready for second stage

Figure 25. Model set, ready for last stage

pulled off when the mould is removed. Now, if the head is divided the other way, with the seam running round the edge of the ears and over the head, this will be better, but the jawline and the underside of the chin will be undercut. To avoid this, the front half of the mould would be made in two, with the seam following the jawline and chin. The nostrils are an impossible problem and would have to be blocked up. For a woman's head there might be the added complications of hair style; a bun, for instance, might mean the back half of the mould would have to be made in two halves.

To decide on the number of pieces in which a mould must be made, and where the seams ought to run, requires considerable deliberation, one must visualize how the pieces of mould will remove without damaging the model, the seams avoiding, if possible, any parts which are modelled in high detail.

Setting up the walls

When the position of the seams has been determined it is helpful to mark them in ink on the clay model. Decide which section must be made first, and enclose it with a wall which is made from a rolled out sheet of clay about ¼" thick. The width of the sheet of clay will vary according to the size of the model, but it will be at least 1" and might be as much as 3" or 4". Fit the wall along the ink line, exactly to the shape of the model, and as far as possible see that it forms a right angle with it. The plaster mould is made only on one side of this wall, and against the other must be placed a roll of clay to act as support along the wall's length. Care must be taken not to damage the model whilst fitting either the wall or the support.

As the next stage involves vigorous handling of plaster it is advisable to protect the surrounding floor and furniture with plenty of newspaper.

Making the mould

Be sure to mix enough plaster for the whole operation (see chapter 3). While it is still fairly liquid put a thin coating all over the enclosed area. Let the plaster dribble down from the top, making sure that it gets into all nooks and crannies. To ensure that every hollow is filled, hold the tips of the fingers on the ball of the thumb, dip them in plaster and flick at the model, shooting plaster into the deepest holes. As the rest of the plaster thickens keep piling it on until it builds up to a thickness of 1″ or 1½″ (or a little thicker for larger moulds). At first the plaster will keep sliding to the bottom, but as it stiffens it will stay in position, after which it is necessary to work fast to finish before it sets too hard.

When the plaster has set, remove the clay walls, neaten the outside edges of the plaster, and with the milled edge of a sixpence, make two or three semi-spherical holes in the smooth edge of this section, providing a key for the next section. Paint soft soap all over the edge, work in well and wipe it off with a small sponge; repeat several times. This closes the pores of the plaster so that the next section will not stick to it. Be careful not to get the clay wet and soapy in the process.

The other sections are made, in turn, in exactly the same way. When the whole is complete scrape down the outside of the seams with a knife until a thin, dark line shows (figures 24 and 25).

Leave the mould for an hour or so to harden, after which it can be taken off the model. Turn the model base upwards, pour a little water on the clay, and try, gently, to push off one section of the mould. If this does not work scoop out some of the clay, without touching the inside of the mould, and pour in some water to swell the clay. Eventually one piece will come away: the rest is simple.

Casting slip

Specially prepared slip, to which a 'deflocculant' has been added, is needed for slip casting. This speeds up the casting process by allowing the slip extra fluidity without the addition of water which both weakens the casting and saturates the mould.

For a good casting slip mix in a dry state, 50 per cent Ball clay, 20 per cent Feldspar, 20 per cent china clay, and 10 per cent Flint. Add 40 per cent (by weight) of water, 0·3 per cent Sodium silicate and 0·3 per cent Soda ash. Allow to soak, and sieve.

Should the beginner be overcome at first by having to cope with all these ingredients or does not have them all on hand but is curious to try before buying them then the following is a simpler recipe. To 10 lb. of dry clay add ½ oz. soda ash and ½ oz. of silicate of soda (waterglass as used for preserving eggs) previously mixed with 3½ pints of warm water. This is really too plastic for casting slip and if it should stick to the mould or crack while drying flint can be added. Even slip used for slip trailing can be tried but it will shrink a great deal.

Making the slip cast

See that the mould is clean and put it together again, tying it firmly with string and forcing small sticks between the string and mould to really tighten it. Elastic bands made from a section of old car inner tube can be used instead. When the mould is quite dried out, wedge it firmly to keep it level and pour the slip in gently to avoid forming bubbles which might clog delicate modelling: to make sure tap the mould so that any present will rise to the surface. As the plaster absorbs water from the slip the level will sink in the middle, so continually top up with more. When the drying slip has begun to form a crust about ½" to ¾" thick, according to the size of the model, tip out the excess. Leave the mould open end downwards, resting on two sticks over a bowl; it will have to stay like this until the clay is sufficiently dry for the mould to be safely removed. The removal must be done carefully, piece by piece. Should it be necessary, either for reasons of strength or of neatness, to fill in the bottom of the model, do so before the mould is removed, using a rolled-out piece of clay made from the slip employed in the casting. Press the new base down a little so that the model is not actually standing on it, for otherwise it might rock. A hole must be made in the base to allow the expanded air to escape during the firing.

The seams on the model, made by the joints in the mould, should be scraped off and any other marks or scrapes generally trimmed. When the mould is dry, the casting process may be repeated.

MOULD MAKING AND SLIP CASTING
FOR POTS

This method is extensively used in the making of domestic ware, and for this the decisions concerning the pieces of the mould are much simpler.

Making the master shape

The master shape has to be made first. It must be solid and can be modelled by hand, but if it is to be circular in plan it is easier to make it on a wheel. To do the latter, make a solid cylinder of clay a little larger than the shape required and let it dry to leather-hardness. Fix this firmly to the wheel, using slurry and scoring the base, and turn the clay to the shape desired (figure 26). A coil may be used for additional support but it must be removed before completing the shape. Although by this time the slurry will have set to form a fairly strong bond, proceed cautiously with the turning.

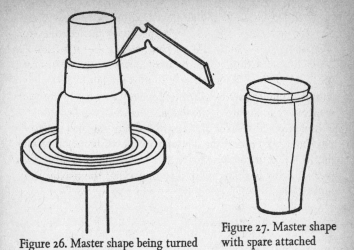

Figure 26. Master shape being turned

Figure 27. Master shape with spare attached

What is called a 'spare' is made in the same way for the top of the shape; this is a flat disc about 2″ thick tapering a little to the bottom, where it is $\frac{1}{8}$″ less in diameter than the top; it is held in place with ordinary dressmaker's pins. This spare provides for an extra flange of clay on the slip cast which is finally trimmed off with a knife; the flange is simply a protection for the proper rim which would otherwise get damaged when the thickness of the drying slip is being tested.

Next draw an ink line vertically bisecting the whole shape, for the pot has to be set horizontally in a bed of clay exactly to this line (figure 27).

Making the mould

For this purpose set the master shape in a block of clay whose width is about 3″ greater than the diameter of the shape at its widest and whose length is that of the pot and spare together. Now scoop out a hollow that allows exactly half the pot to rise above the flat surface. A piece of thin paper (hard toilet-paper does very well) should be placed in the hollow to protect the surface of the master shape. It is not necessary for the hollow to be exactly the shape of the pot, but it must hold it firmly in position, precisely at right angles where it meets the block surface. This first operation is the most difficult yet the most important; it must be done very accurately without damaging the surface of the shape.

Build up walls (made of glass, tiles, or any smooth surfaced, rigid material) round the block at least $1\frac{1}{2}''$ higher than the pot in order to contain the plaster to be poured over it; the corners must be sealed with clay to prevent the plaster leaking out (figure 28).

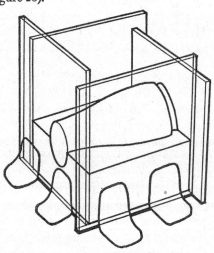

Figure 28. Master shape set, ready for first section

Pour plaster over the pot and leave it to set for about ten minutes before removing the walls and the clay block. The pot is now set in a block of plaster. Notches must be made in this block, two on each side of the pot, to make a key for the second piece of the mould. This is done and the block subse-

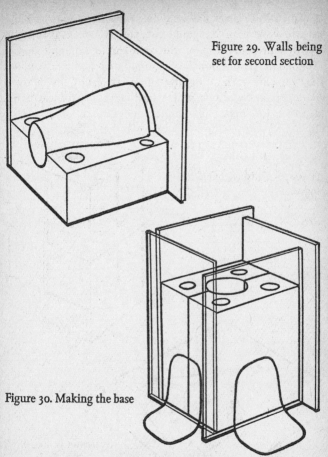

Figure 29. Walls being set for second section

Figure 30. Making the base

quently soaped in exactly the same way as for the mould previously described, after which the walls are reset and the second piece made (figure 29). To make the base set the whole mould bottom end up, make more notches and soap the surface, replacing the walls before pouring for the third piece (figure 30).

When the plaster has firmly set (about one hour) remove the three pieces of the mould from the clay shape. If this is at all difficult pour water on the open end to expand the clay. The mould should now be thoroughly washed, reassembled, tied together with string or stout elastic bands, and allowed to dry for a day or two, after which it is ready for use (figure 31).

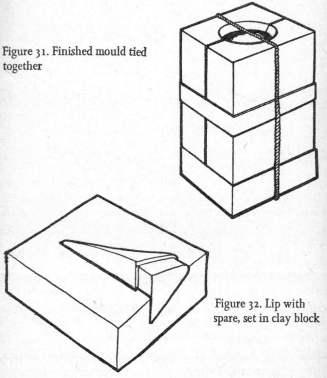

Figure 31. Finished mould tied together

Figure 32. Lip with spare, set in clay block

Handles, spouts and lips of jugs or teapots are best made separately, modelled, moulded and cast in exactly the same way (figures 32 and 33). Such an attachment is affixed to the

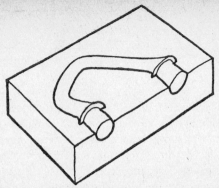

Figure 33. Handle with spares set in clay block

main shape when both are in a leather-hard condition. It is also possible to pull handles manually, and use them with cast ware.

Pottery made in this way has its own character, one quite different from that resulting from methods of hand building or throwing. Cast ware is harder in feel, more mechanical, less likely to have technical imperfection, but a little less personal. Plate 44 shows an excellent eighteenth-century jug whose vertical ribs could have been made on the original master shape or later carved into the plaster mould. Plate 45 shows a good twentieth-century example in which the decoration is unusually personal. Both are beautiful in their own way, and both illustrate the delicate, finished, yet slightly colder character of this kind of work.

Conclusion

IT is no good pretending that the twentieth-century potter can use clay in some entirely new way: any area into which he moves will have been explored before. Ancient civilizations modelled pottery for amusement, for use as children's toys and as jewellery, and explored most of the fundamental shapes suitable for the functions of pottery; the Saracens designed tiles so expertly as to make them the whole basis of their architectural decoration; Della Robbia made superb modelled plaques in the fifteenth century, but they were by no means the first.

Since the craft movement, inspired by William Morris and others in the nineteenth century, attempted to rediscover a lost standard, many potters have quite consciously returned to the styles of earlier epochs, including the primitive periods, for inspiration. It is quite noticeable that many older modern potters are strongly influenced by the forms of Chinese Sung, Japanese and Korean, and English Medieval Pottery. Work derived from African sources has generally not been so good. The younger generation has been struggling hard to be less immediately derivative, and sometimes has succeeded.

This does not mean that nothing new is possible: in art there are always new ways of looking at old themes; there is always the development of different styles as well as the individual working in a style, but with his own unique touch. Some contemporary abstract modelling is not quite like anything done before in history; a good deal of modern Finnish pottery has very much its own character. Infinite variation within apparently small limits; that is the fascination.

Primitive pottery, of course, was all functional. Every piece had a use of some sort or other. But, already, in some of the ancient civilizations, pottery had acquired the kind of status of high art, in which a pot might be considered as a significant aesthetic object in itself, not necessarily made either primarily or at all for use. It is no good ignoring this fact.

So, whereas we have been somewhat critical of Classical Greek work, particularly of the way in which it was painted, it can be instanced as pottery which was almost always designed for a specific purpose. Arthur Lane, in his book *Greek Pottery*,* has strongly made the point that the different shapes were all designed for their specific functions. This is not necessarily the case, as he notes, with the Chinese Sung pottery which we have praised for other reasons. In fact, although some of this was made for a function, some could only be used for displaying flowers, and there are pieces for which even this would seem to be too vulgar an idea. They exist, strongly, just to be themselves for as long as possible. Since industry produces the bulk of all functional work, the studio potter has more time (if he can sell his work) to concentrate on the pot as a pot. And this, it must be supposed, is only natural and legitimate: as we have seen, an empty pot can be a fine thing to have about.

Yet to some experienced potters, as well as beginners there is a quite overwhelming excitement in making things that they will use constantly afterwards: it is not exaggerating to say that many find that this work has real therapeutic value. It is a good idea, therefore, for a beginner to range as wide as possible both in non-functional and functional work. Casseroles, coffee jugs, soup dishes, teapots, chess sets – all can be made for one's own use (plate 46).

It is wise, too, to experiment technically as broadly as possible; by doing so you will find the fields in which you have a

* *Greek Pottery*, by Arthur Lane. Faber & Faber.

special ability. Plate 18 shows the work of an amateur who discovered a natural talent for slip decoration and whose work is quite up to professional standard. Try small- and large-scale work. For just as some sculptors work much better at a large-scale, others in miniature, potters can be the same – one succeeding with bold generous pots, another with delicate modelling. In decoration one may be spontaneous and broad, another slow and fine. When you have explored thoroughly you may like to specialize. Indeed, many professional potters, the longer they practice, become interested in one or two aspects of the craft, or have long periods in which a particular shape, or a method of glazing or decorating may occupy them exclusively.

Appendix 1.

The Use of Oxides for Colouring

BLUE

Cobalt oxide

Blue slip: 1–3 per cent cobalt oxide gives bright mid-blue – dark blue

FOR PAINTED DECORATION Cobalt oxide is excellent for painting on unfired clay or tin glaze. On biscuit it tends to run and spread at the edges because it acts as a flux with glaze.

Blue glaze: ¼ to 1 per cent cobalt oxide gives mid-strong blue. This rather obvious blue can be varied by adding small quantities of Iron Oxide or Manganese Oxide.

GENERAL REMARKS Cobalt oxide has relatively large particles and will give a speckled effect, especially to slip, unless well ground before use.

Other blues: underglaze colour – glaze stain – body stain.

GREEN

Copper Oxide

Green slip: 3 per cent copper oxide gives mid-green

FOR PAINTED DECORATION Copper oxide gives a good natural green on biscuit or tin glaze.

Green glaze: 1 to 3 per cent copper oxide gives a light to strong green. The addition of a little cobalt oxide gives a blue-green.

GENERAL REMARKS If more than 5 per cent copper oxide is used in glaze or slip it will lose its greenness and turn a metallic black when fired.

It is rather volatile and may stain pots placed near it in the kiln.

Other greens: underglaze colour. Any green containing

chromium oxide may tinge tin glaze pink in the firing. Glaze stain – body stain.

YELLOW

Yellow is a difficult colour to produce with basic oxides especially for a transparent glaze.

Lead antimoniate

Slip: Does not produce a very satisfactory yellow slip.

FOR PAINTED DECORATION Excellent for painting on tin glaze. Not suitable for painting on biscuit because it does not give a strong enough colour.

Yellow glaze: Up to 10 per cent can be added to a transparent glaze. More will begin to make it opaque. It is not very stable in leadless glazes.

Other yellows: underglaze colour – glaze stain – body stain.

RED

There is no basic oxide which gives scarlet or crimson reds for glaze, slip or painted decoration. There are red-prepared stains for glazes and clay and these will give oranges, pinks, but usually nothing stronger. Underglaze colour ranges usually include a crimson as well.

BROWN

Iron oxide and manganese oxide.

Iron oxide gives warm tan-coloured browns and is very useful for modifying the tints of other colours, and manganese oxide gives a cooler purplish range.

Slip: 2 to 6 per cent iron oxide gives light tan – dark rich brown. 3 to 6 per cent manganese gives varying shades of cool brown.

FOR PAINTED DECORATION Iron and manganese oxides are both useful colours for painted decoration. The iron oxide tends to be dissolved by lead glazes, particularly, and should be used fairly thickly.

Both oxides are excellent for painting on tin glaze.

Glaze: 2 to 5 per cent iron oxide gives amber to dark brown.

2 to 4 per cent manganese oxide gives light to dark purply-brown.

Other Browns: underglaze colour – glaze stain – body stain.

BLACK

Blacks are made by mixing manganese, cobalt and iron oxides. The following proportions suggested for each may have to be adjusted.

Black slip: 2 per cent manganese oxide

3 per cent iron oxide

2 per cent cobalt oxide

FOR PAINTED DECORATION Various mixtures of basic oxides as given for slip or glaze.

Black glaze: 8 per cent manganese oxide

4 per cent iron oxide

2 per cent cobalt oxide

Other blacks: underglaze colour – glaze stains – body stain.

OTHER COLOURS

Any of the metal oxides can be mixed together to form variations on their basic colours. Some of the more subtle coloured glazes are made by adding three different oxides, care has to be taken not to add too great a proportion of oxides to glaze as many of them are fluxes and will alter the maturing temperature.

Appendix 2.

Some Manufacturers of Potters' Materials and Equipment

Wengers
Etruria
Stoke-on-Trent.

All potters' materials and equipment.

Potclays Ltd
Wharf House
Copeland Street
Stoke-on-Trent.

Potters' materials.

Podmore and Sons Ltd
Shelton
Stoke-on-Trent.

All potters' materials and equipment.

Fulham Pottery
New Kings Road
London S.W.6.

All potters' materials and equipment.

Mills and Hubball Ltd
Victoria Rise
North Side
Clapham Common
London S.W.4.

All potters' materials and equipment.

Cromartie Kilns
Dividy Road
Longton
Staffordshire.

Electric kilns.

Catterson-Smith
Exhibition Road
Wembley.

Electric kilns and wheels.

Grafton Kilns   Electric kilns
The Allied Heat Co.
Elecfurn Works
Otterspool Way
Watford By-Pass
Watford
Hertfordshire.

Potters Equipment Co.   Wheels.
73–77 Britannia Road
London S.W.6.

Catalogue of Illustrations

1. Raku tea bowl. Soft earthenware. Hand built. *British Museum, London* (Photograph reproduced by permission of the Trustees of the British Museum, London).
2. Coiled pot. Stoneware. By student of the Farnham School of Art.
3. Coiled pots. Stoneware decorated with black and white glazes. Modern. By recreational student of the Farnham School of Art.
4. Coiled pot. Terra-cotta with impressed decoration. Modern African.
5. Slab pot. Stoneware. Modern. By student of the Farnham School of Art.
6. Slab pots. Stoneware. Modern. By Paul Brown and Alan Wallwork.
7. Pressed dishes. Earthenware decorated with trailed slip. Modern. By recreational student of the Farnham School of Art.
8. Hand built pot. Unglazed earthenware with carved decoration. Aztec. *Horniman Museum, London.*
9. Thrown jug. Earthenware with carved decoration and turquoise glaze. Persian. Early thirteenth century. *Victoria and Albert Museum, London.* (Victoria and Albert Museum. Crown Copyright.)
10. Thrown jug. Earthenware with sgraffito decoration in cream and dark brown. Staffordshire. *Victoria and Albert Museum, London.* (Victoria and Albert Museum. Crown Copyright.)
11. Thrown bread bin. Red earthenware with raised decoration. Modern. By Georgia Naylor.
12. Thrown storage jars. Grey-blue earthenware with white lettering. Modern. By Peter Wright. *Anschel shop.*
13. Thrown dishes. Blue-grey earthenware with white decoration. Left, stencil method. Modern. By Wendy Norland, *Heal's.*

14. Cast jug. Cream earthenware decorated in black with an engraving. Nineteenth century. *Victoria and Albert Museum, London.* (Victoria and Albert Museum. Crown Copyright.)

15. Attic red figured hydria. Greek *c.* 410 B.C. *British Museum, London.* (Photograph reproduced by permission of the Trustees of the British Museum, London.)

16. Sgraffito decorated earthenware plate. White slip over brown. English seventeenth century. *Victoria and Albert Museum, London.* (Victoria and Albert Museum. Crown Copyright.)

17. Slip trailed decoration light and dark brown and cream. ware. Spanish plate. Sixteenth century. *Victoria and Albert Museum, London.* (Victoria and Albert Museum. Crown Copyright.)

18. Slip trailed decoration white on dark brown. Modern English plate. By a student of Isleworth Technical College.

19. Black underglaze painted on earthenware. Persian bowl thirteenth century. *Victoria and Albert Museum, London.* (Victoria and Albert Museum. Crown Copyright.)

20. Blue underglaze painted on white tin glaze, earthenware. Spanish plate. Early twentieth century. *Victoria and Albert Museum, London.* (Victoria and Albert Museum. Crown Copyright).

21. Blue underglaze and lustre painted on tin glaze, earthenware. Spanish plate. Sixteenth century. *Victoria and Albert Museum, London.* (Victoria and Albert Museum. Crown Copyright.)

22. Blue, green and orange painted on tin glaze, earthenware. Lambeth plate. Seventeenth century. *Victoria and Albert Museum, London.* (Victoria and Albert Museum. Crown Copyright.)

23. Mixing bowl. Purple brown on buff unglazed earthenware. Greek 1375–1200 B.C. *British Museum, London.* (Photograph reproduced by permission of the Trustees of the British Museum, London.)

24. Plaque. Brown underglaze painted on cream, earthenware. By Sidney Irwin.

25. Detail of brushwork on Sung vase. Stoneware.

26. Detail of brushwork on twentieth-century Spanish dish.

27. Detail of brushwork on seventeenth-century Lambeth dish.

28. Stoneware vase, green glaze mottled with dark blue. Kwantung. Probably eighteenth century. *Victoria and Albert Museum, London.* (Victoria and Albert Museum. Crown Copyright.)

29. Korean stoneware vase. Dark brown painted on cream. *British Museum, London.* (Photograph reproduced by permission of the Trustees of the British Museum, London.)

30. Sung stoneware jar. Thick lavender-blue glaze with red markings. A.D. 960–1279. *Victoria and Albert Museum, London.* (Victoria and Albert Museum. Crown Copyright.)

31. Sung stoneware vase. Black glaze. A.D. 960–1279. *Victoria and Albert Museum, London.* (Victoria and Albert Museum. Crown Copyright.)

32. Sung stoneware vase. Cream with dark brown decoration. A.D. 960–1297. *Victoria and Albert Museum, London.* (Victoria and Albert Museum. Crown Copyright.)

33. Black and rust stoneware pot. Modern. By Paul Barron.

34. Stoneware bottles with coloured glazes. Modern. By Paul Barron.

35. Stoneware vase. Stoneware bowl. Painted in blue and cream glaze. By Henry Hammond.

36. Stoneware vase. Buff with white glaze. Modern. By Joan Kidman.

37. Buff earthenware pot painted in black and red brown. Chinese neolithic. *Victoria and Albert Museum, London.* (Victoria and Albert Museum. Crown Copyright.)

38. Chinese Amphora. *British Museum, London.* (Photograph reproduced by permission of the Trustees of the British Museum, London.)

39. Detail of handles of Sung jar illustrated in plate 30.

40. Salt-glaze group of Virgin and child. 1760 English. *The Royal Pavilion, Brighton.*

41. Man on horseback and a Lady. Eighteenth century. *Victoria and Albert Museum, London.* (Victoria and Albert Museum. Crown Copyright.)

42. Cat in unglazed cream earthenware decorated with light red.

Modern. By Mary Lambert. Fish in dark green earthenware with impressed decoration. Modern. By Sidney Irwin.

43. Guarding Lion. Earthenware, painted on red pigment. Chinese A.D. 220–599 *Victoria and Albert Museum, London.* (Victoria and Albert Museum. Crown Copyright.)

44. Factory made earthenware jug. Staffordshire 1790. *Victoria and Albert Museum, London.* (Victoria and Albert Museum. Crown Copyright.)

45. White earthenware slip-cast vase. Modern. By R. Mitchell.

46. An assortment of domestic pottery. By Students of the Hammersmith College of Art.

Bibliography

Billington, Dora, *The Technique of Pottery*, Batsford
Clarke, Kenneth, *Practical Pottery and Ceramics*, Studio Vista
Fieldhouse, Murray, *Pottery*, A Foyles Handbook
Honey, William Bowyer, *The Art of the Potter*, Faber & Faber
Lane, Arthur, *Greek Pottery*, Faber & Faber
Leach, Bernard, *A Potter's Book*, Faber & Faber
Rackham, Bernard, *Early Staffordshire Pottery*, Faber & Faber
Rhodes, Daniel, *Clay and Glazes for the Potter*, Pitman
Rosenthal, Ernst, *Pottery and Ceramics*, Penguin Books
Tyler, Keith, *Pottery without a Wheel*, The Dryad Press
Wren, Denise and Rosemary, *Pottery Making*, Pitman

Index

NOTES